P9-EDH-842

WITHDRAWN

E
169.12
F76

Frost, David
The Americans

DATE DUE

JUN 16 71		
NOV 3 71		
NOV 24 71		
FEB 7 73		

LENDING POLICY
IF YOU DAMAGE OR LOSE LIBRARY
MATERIALS, THEN YOU WILL BE
CHARGED FOR REPLACEMENT. FAIL-
URE TO PAY AFFECTS LIBRARY
PRIVILEGES, GRADES, TRANSCRIPTS,
DIPLOMAS, AND REGISTRATION
PRIVILEGES OR ANY COMBINATION
THEREOF.

The Americans

DAVID FROST *The*

Americans

STEIN AND DAY/*Publishers*/New York
𝔰𝔇

First published in 1970
Copyright © 1970 David Frost
Library of Congress Catalog Card No. 70-126998
All rights reserved
Published simultaneously in Canada by Saunders of Toronto Ltd
Designed by David Miller
Printed in the United States of America
Stein and Day/*Publishers*/7 East 48 Street, New York, N.Y. 10017
SBN 8128-1334-0

Contents

◆

Race: Everybody Wins or Everybody Loses

Women in Revolt

Kids in Revolt

The Political Crafts

Thank You

◆

I am in debt to so many people.

To Peter Baker, Neil Shand, Bob Carman, and the whole of my production team at the Little Theatre, off Times Square, to Billy Taylor, and to Vincent Sardi for providing spiritual inspiration next door.

To Chet Collier and everyone at Group W—Don McGannon, Marv Shapiro, Dave Henderson, and many more—for making things happen in the first place. (Assuming for a moment that that is not billing to which my mother feels herself entitled.)

To all those who figure in this book, for their time and their thoughts, and their wit and their warmth.

And to you, gentle reader. For reading the book, assuming, of course, that you are about to, and for watching the show, assuming, of course, that you have!

DAVID FROST
The Little Theatre
September 1, 1970

The Americans

The Americans Need No Introduction

◆

INVITED TO WRITE, as a sequel to *The English,* a book to be called *The Americans,* I at once declined.

After all, I had lived in England for twenty-eight summers (using the word in its most generous sense) when I wrote *The English* with Antony Jay. Since America is four times as big and I first came here back in 1963, by a similar time scale I would be qualified to write *The Americans* by June 2075.

Mind you, though, even in a comparatively brief and, on my side at any rate, rapturous acquaintance, seven years is still long enough to have compiled quite a mini-gallery of Americana to cherish, starting with softshell crabs, cheesecake, and French toast (never to be seen in France any more than English muffins are to be seen in England), and progressing through the little civilities of life in America (yes, civilities) like getting a book of matches free with a pack of cigarettes.

These are some of the delights of my early visits to America. There are many more. The New York cab drivers can be as Runyonesque as they are supposed to be. I remember being in a cab once on a boiling July day. We were stuck in a traffic jam. Ten minutes passed and we did not move. We sat and sweltered. I bore it in silence, because there just seemed to be no words to express our misery. The driver found them. "Better maybe we never *invented* the wheel, huh?" he said.

And where else but in America, I think, would you have seen the Park Avenue tableau that was enacted early every morning during that massively heavy snowfall one winter, when the residents were out on the street shaking the snow from frail branches in order that they wouldn't snap under the weight.

Where else but in America could there be signs in restaurants saying, "Don't forget! Buy your mother a dinner on May 11."

Where but in America would a young secretary become so bemused by the all-embracing Western décor of a bar that, having excused herself from the table, she would return a couple of minutes later and say somewhat embarrassedly, "David, am I a heifer or a steer?"

Where else but in America, maybe, signs like the one I noted on Interstate Highway 95: "He who has one for the road gets a trooper for a chaser."

Almost as special were the two lacquered ladies from Long Island whom Peter Baker overheard in Sardi's two days after Neil Armstrong walked on the moon. "What a week," said one. "Absolutely nothing happened." "What do you mean, 'nothing happened?'" the friend protested. "Don't you realize that three Americans have flown to the moon, around the moon, and written an indelible page in the history books by landing on the moon?" "So?" said the first lady. "If you have money you travel."

Where but in America could I meet someone like the Reverend Robert Truesdell, who conducts eighty or ninety marriages on a good Friday and Saturday night in Las Vegas. "We in the marriage industry . . ." he said.

And maybe only in somewhere like Houston could one hear a visionary industrialist boom, pointing proudly at the Astroturf, "We have made grass obsolete."

And where else but in America could an Englishman get off a plane and be given the heartwarming greeting, "Hello, David, it must be nice to be home again."

Yes, madam, I must say it feels that way.

It was from musings like these that I realized that *The Americans* did not have to be written. It already had been, not by me alone—far from it—but, between my questions and their answers, by us—by the multitude of Americans of every generation, stars and unknowns, who have talked with me on my television program. They, much better than I, will tell you about the Americans.

For Americans do not suffer from that occasional English affliction—the stiff uncommunicative upper lip. They respond so quickly to anyone with a genuine interest in them; if you really *want* to know what makes an American tick, he will tell you as openly and honestly as he can. Candor, I often think, is second nature, and nobody has talked to me more vividly and positively than my American friends. Arthur Godfrey was on television when he said, "Do you want to know a secret?" In front of millions of people he proceeded to tell us. Angelica Huston, having just played her first starring role in a movie, directed by her father John Huston, was also on television when she said with captivating directness: "I don't really think I've done him justice, and I'm very sorry about it. There were so many young girls waiting for the opportunity. Dying for it. And it was handed to me on a plate! It really shocks me to look at myself and see that I went into it without the preparation that I should have had. I shouldn't have been that selfish. I think I shouldn't have taken it."

Remarks that might have an overemotional ring about them elsewhere sound perfectly "right." "This country gave me everything I have. I was a little immigrant kid from Rumania. My father was a pushcart peddler. And here I became a Justice of the Supreme Court because of the opportunities this glorious country of ours gives every man," Judge Samuel Leibowitz once said—not in a ringing courtroom speech but almost casually, during a conversation on the air.

It will be apparent that my purpose here is not to be a critic of America, nor a pundit about it: my purpose in this book as on television is to *listen* to America. I hope that you will find what follows a kaleidoscope—of people and of attitudes and of ideologies, maybe sometimes in direct or indirect conflict one with the other.

13

It would have been possible, of course, to recast our conversations into a more "literary" form. But I much prefer to have you read them as they happened, with all the diversity of style and emphasis that makes the Americans, for me, endlessly fascinating.

THE CRAFTSY ARTS

◆

THERE REALLY is no business like it. Any time, anywhere around the world, that a man sets out a few rows of chairs, hangs up a white sheet, turns down the lights, switches on a projector, and keeps a few hundred of his fellow men enthralled for a couple of hours, the Americans will be gratefully saluted for having invented it—the best, the biggest, the most delightful business of them all: show business. The gentle art of making other people temporarily happy.

We talk about America as the melting pot, and one example of how the process works is that, with no one single cultural activity to claim as their own speciality, the Americans melted the whole lot down—singing, dancing, acting, writing, painting, telling jokes, and doing tricks—and produced the movies; thereby giving the rest of us endless hours of innocent pleasure (not to mention somewhere cosier than a public park bench to conduct the uneasy overtures to our very first love affairs).

Of course, although people sometimes wonder whether America invented Hollywood or whether Hollywood invented America, show business is not just the movies. I am pretty sure that the first four words the human race really put together when we came down out of the trees all those centuries ago were, "Tell us a story." And show business is what happens whenever someone, in answer to that most human little plea, gets a crowd together and begins his story. Words

15

or music; books, pictures, stage, screen, radio or television—what they are all saying is, "Gather ye round and enjoy yourselves for a while."

It's a magic that anyone who has ever been on a stage or in front of an audience knows about. The magic to which Jackie Gleason was referring when he told me about his first stage appearance in a school play.

"It was the graduation play in Public School 73, and I was doing a take-off on Little Red Riding Hood, and during the motions that I made I knocked the microphone off, which was a wooden microphone, it was a make-believe microphone, and the principal picked it up and put it back on the stage and I said, 'That's the first thing you've ever done for the kids.' It got a big laugh from the kids, not a very big laugh from him. And that's when I got the bug. You know all you have to do is hear one laugh."

So let us begin with perhaps the most varied, the most motley collection of talents we shall meet in the course of the book. The author, the playwright, the television star, the young hero and the great lady of the stage, not to mention the virtuosos of the trumpet, the piano, and whatever Orson Welles is currently turning his talents to!

In short, some of the Americans who are entertaining audiences in America today . . .

When Does a Writer Become a Star?

◆

Truman Capote

FROST: About a year ago I was talking to Noel Coward, and I asked him at what age he knew that he was a star, and he said, "Two!" You're a star. At what age did you realize that you were a star-writer personality?

CAPOTE: You've got to separate those two things. A personality or a writer?

FROST: Well, you're a mixture of the two, aren't you?

CAPOTE: Well, I realized that I could get away with murder when I was about six.

FROST: Really?

CAPOTE: In school.

FROST: What sort of things could you get away with?

CAPOTE: Well, all the teachers thought that I was much brighter than I was. And so I could get away with anything— if that's what you mean, having a sort of certainty of your own ability to do a thing.

FROST: What was your first great coup? The first thing you really got away with?

CAPOTE: I guess maybe I didn't really mean it in that sense, but the first thing that happened to me in my career that gave me a sense of confidence—because, you see, I didn't finish high school. I didn't want to because I had begun to publish stories when I was fourteen, fifteen, and I wanted to come to live in New York, and I was living in New Orleans. And I came to work with the *New Yorker* magazine. But they didn't know how old I was. I mean, I'd been sending them

17

material and stories and things and I actually was about seventeen years old, and I came up to New York. They had written me a letter and said they would be very pleased to give me an interview to work there as a reporter. And so I arrived, and I was taken to see the managing editor, who is now the editor of the *New Yorker,* and when I was seventeen I looked about ten years old. And this man nearly fainted. And so I said, "But I've come all the way from New Orleans." He said, "But we can't do this—it's child labor. We can't send you out to interview anybody." But in the end they let me stay, and I had a job there, and I worked there for two years, until I published a book.

FROST: Between the age of six, when you realized you could get away with anything, and the age of seventeen, you had lots of other ambitions, didn't you? You wanted to be a tap dancer?

(*Laughter*)

CAPOTE: Oh, that's just something I put in *Who's Who.*

FROST: It's not true?

CAPOTE: No. You know, they send you these forms to fill out, what you wanted to do or be in *Who's Who in America,* and I just sent them back a sort of a joke thing. I said that I painted on glass and wrote political speeches and wanted to be a tap dancer, but it was none of it true.

FROST: Well, how do we know that the other story you just told us is true?

CAPOTE: Maybe it isn't. (*Laughter, applause*)

FROST: But what about the rumor that you also had said that you were desperate to learn to play the guitar and learn a song called "I Wish I Were Single Again"? Did you do that, or did you make that up?

CAPOTE: No, I did do that, but that's the only song I ever did learn. I got so tired of that guitar I left it in the bus station in Mobile, Alabama.

FROST: Were you a lovable child?

CAPOTE: Those who knew me well thought so. Those who didn't, no.

18

FROST: Why? Because you were daunting first time out?

CAPOTE: I had a sharp tongue.

FROST: You haven't lost it. You said on one occasion, in fact, that you'd developed the muscles of a veritable barracuda in dealing with your enemies. What bit of dealing with your enemies are you proudest of?

CAPOTE: Doing in Kenneth Tynan. Remember when I had my feud with Kenneth Tynan?

FROST: Over *In Cold Blood*? What was it that really convinced you you'd succeeded in doing him in?

CAPOTE: Because my reply was much better than his attack.

FROST: Have you always been superstitious?

CAPOTE: Yes, but not any more. I was until about ten years ago. I was very interested in horoscopes and things like that, and just one day I took all of them and tore them up, and I'm not going to let myself be victimized by this junk any longer.

FROST: But you had some marvelous superstitions. Half of them you invented yourself, didn't you?

CAPOTE: Oh, yes. I only have one with which I still drive people crazy. I won't have three cigarettes in the same ashtray. I keep taking them out and putting them in my pockets and all over my suit, just so I never have more than two cigarette butts in other people's. I won't let other people have it either. And they keep saying, "What are you doing?"

FROST: Have you any spare cigarette butts with you now?

CAPOTE: No, no, no. I just changed my suit.

FROST: At one stage you always said that you didn't like to travel on an airplane with two nuns?

CAPOTE: I still wouldn't do that. (*Laughter*) I wouldn't go anywhere with two nuns.

FROST: Were you afraid of being hijacked to the Vatican or what? (*Laughter*)

CAPOTE: Maybe there's just something gloomy about it.

FROST: What about *three* nuns?

CAPOTE: Oh, I wouldn't do that either.

FROST: How would you feel about one nun?

CAPOTE: That's all right. (*Laughter*)

FROST: You also had a thing about phone numbers at one time.

CAPOTE: Recently I had a very bad automobile accident, and I hit a tree at forty miles an hour. I went through the windshield. And I was lying on the ground there waiting for the ambulance, and it took about thirty-five minutes before it got there. And during that whole time I was completely conscious. But all that was going through my mind was old telephone numbers. I kept thinking of a telephone and thinking, "Who does that telephone number belong to?" It was a very curious thing, but I entertained and occupied myself, and felt no pain the whole time.

FROST: Really? But before that you found certain combinations of numbers unlucky, didn't you?

CAPOTE: Yes, well, I won't dial them. I had a great fight once with Tennessee Williams. We went to Capri together. This was a long time ago, fifteen years ago. And we went to this hotel, and when they brought the keys with the numbers on them, I looked at my number and I didn't like it. I said to Tennessee, "Would you mind if I had your room and you gave me your key?" And he said, "All right." I went upstairs, and then I came down. We were having a drink, and he walked into the bar with a terrible look on his face, and said—because he's even more superstitious than I am— he said, "I just figured out why you wanted me to have that number instead of you: because it adds up to thirteen."

FROST: What did he do?

CAPOTE: He was furious with me. He said I had no right to put this jinx on him.

FROST: What about the stars and astrology? You believed in those at one stage?

CAPOTE: Not any more.

FROST: Why not? You just decided to chuck them out of the window? What about the belief in God? You said on

20

one occasion that for you art really took the place of religion. Do you believe in a god?

CAPOTE: Not in that specific sense. What I meant when I said I believed in art as a religion is that art can be a comfort and a guide in the passage through life. Art is a recompense for the difficulties of simply living.

FROST: What do you believe in the strongest?

CAPOTE: Art.

FROST: Anything else?

CAPOTE: Friendship.

FROST: Which is more powerful, do you think—friendship or love?

CAPOTE: Friendship. Actually, I think friendship and love are exactly the same thing.

FROST: How do you mean?

CAPOTE: Obviously sex is not love. It's a temporary situation, isn't it? Sex can lead to love, but friendship, real friendship, inevitably leads to love. There can't be any friendship unless it's a real friendship, but then, one doesn't have that many friends in a lifetime.

FROST: Have you ever been in love?

CAPOTE: Oh, yes.

FROST: Often?

CAPOTE: No. Twice.

FROST: And was it just like heightened friendship then?

CAPOTE: Yes. (*Laughter*)

FROST: Heightened in what way?

CAPOTE: Well, I didn't have to finish sentences.

FROST: That's a great definition. But if friendship leads to love, does it normally lead to sex too?

CAPOTE: No.

FROST: You don't seem to have a very high opinion of sex.

CAPOTE: Well, that's not true either. I just don't see in what connection this really falls, because you see I don't think sex has anything to do with friendship. It's very difficult to have a sort of sexual relationship with somebody who

21

actually is a friend. Because there's a kind of tension and antagonism that goes on in a sexual relationship that's the antithesis of friendship, because friendship is the perfect sort of trust and belief and not lying to one another. People who are having a love-sex relationship are continuously lying to each other because the very nature of the relationship demands that they do, because you have to make a love object of this person, which means that you editorialize about them. You know? You cut out what you don't want to see, you add this if it isn't there. And so therefore you're building a lie. But in a friendship you don't do that. You do exactly the reverse. You try more and more to be as completely pure and straight as you can be.

FROST: Have you found you've had more sex relationships than love relationships, or less?

CAPOTE: No, I've had more love relationships than sex relationships.

FROST: But you've only had two love relationships.

CAPOTE: Yes. No, wait— (*Laughter, applause*) Pretty good, pretty good, but you didn't quite get away with it. Let's see now. Let's really figure this out. I tell you what. I've never been to a psychoanalyst, but after this I'll go and consult one, and then I'll have him call you up, and then maybe he can tell you the whole situation.

FROST: More, then, not less.

CAPOTE: I'm going to leave it to the analyst.

FROST: You once said, "Sex is like sneezing."

CAPOTE: Yes. I meant that literally. I was making a metaphor for orgasm. What is the nearest thing in physical sensation to an orgasm? And I came up with the idea that it was sneezing. (*Laughter*)

FROST: You also said once, when you were analyzing whether you would have gone to a psychiatrist, that it might "have lessened the penalties I pay." I can't imagine you ever paying penalties. Have you?

CAPOTE: Sure, everybody pays penalties.

FROST: What sort of people pay?

22

CAPOTE: In the process of maturing, if you mature at all, one has to pay a certain price.

FROST: What do you mean?

CAPOTE: I don't think it's possible to go through life, unless you're a complete idiot, without being continuously hurt one way or another. The only thing that doesn't hurt me is to pick up a newspaper and read some libelous thing about me or some bad review of something. That doesn't bother me at all. But if I feel somebody has betrayed me in some way or been disloyal about something, I get terribly upset about it.

FROST: You said once the only thing you hate reading about yourself in the papers is the truth.

CAPOTE: That's it.

FROST: The lies are fine?

CAPOTE: I don't care what anybody says about me as long as it isn't true. (*Laughter and applause*)

Can a Martian Survive by Pretending to Be
a Leading American Actor?

◆

Orson Welles

FROST: Is it really true that you never see your own pic
tures after you've finished them?

WELLES: I know it sounds like a terrible pose, but it's
really a neurosis, I suppose.

FROST: Why don't you see them afterward, to swell with
pride or—

WELLES: Because they're on film, in a tin can, and they
can never be changed.

FROST: And if you saw them—

WELLES: For example, if you direct a play, it's opened,
and you see it again after it's been running awhile, and you
don't like it too well, you can take the cast and say, "Well,
we'll have a rehearsal tomorrow, we'll rewrite that scene,
we'll play that a little differently," but a movie is locked up
forever. You can always do it better. But you can't change
a finished movie.

FROST: You said once that you'd been "seduced away from
politics by the movies." Do you still wish you'd been in politics?

WELLES: I suppose that only very intelligent people don't
wish they were in politics, and I'm dumb enough to want to
be in there.

FROST: And why do you want to be in?

WELLES: Well, you know, you always think that you might
be able to help a little. I suppose it's just an ego trip. It is
like an audience in a theater that sees an actor and says, "I

24

could do that pretty well, too." An actor sees a congressman and says the same thing. Of course, you've got a few actors in politics now.

FROST: You want to go on?

WELLES: Ask the students in California to fill in.

FROST: Do you share the feelings of the students, in fact? When you were young you said that the youth in America could demand anything. Do you think young people demand too much?

WELLES: No, certainly not. There isn't a specific virtue in being young. What is right about them is that they're demanding what we should have had a long time ago. They may be making some mistakes, but they are mistakes of tactics and strategy, not of human feeling. The hopeful thing is that maybe a generation as alert and alive as it is may bring some changes. We'd better see them quick, because things are going to get worse than they are now.

FROST: What are your predictions about our future? You've got a sort of predictive power, haven't you? Didn't you once predict, for instance, Oona Chaplin was going to marry Charlie Chaplin before she even met him?

WELLES: Yes, but politics is tougher than marriage.

FROST: How did you know that?

WELLES: It was one of those guesses. I suppose Oona looked like the kind of girl that would be happy with Charlie, and instead of thinking, "Maybe you'll meet him," I just twitted her and said, "You're going to marry him," and she did. But you asked me about a political prediction and I couldn't make one.

FROST: What's the last premonition you had?

WELLES: I like to forget them, like my movies.

FROST: Which one are you proudest of, the best one?

WELLES: Oh, let's change the subject. I don't want to clam up and spoil the show. I'll answer anything you want but don't ask me "proudest" or anything like that. I like to think that my films are so much better than they were, you know, and I say, "Oh, that great movie." But if I'd have to see it,

I'd find out that maybe some of those bad notices were right.

FROST: But do you think you've achieved great things in your life, or do you not even like to think of it?

WELLES: You know, we've only got so much energy to go on, and I think it's a waste of energy. I think that's a consolation for real old age.

FROST: It was in Ireland that you started acting, wasn't it?

WELLES: Yes, that was to get out of school. I had a scholarship for Harvard. I'm a dropout. I'd been painting in Ireland, and it got to be winter, and the days were getting short and so was my money, and I knew I was going to have to go back to America to a dreaded school of learning. So I went backstage at the Gate Theatre and told them I was a famous star from the New York Theatre Guild and just for the fun of it I'd like to stay with them and play a few leading roles.

Now, you can only do that if you don't believe that it matters, if you don't care. I had no desire to be an actor. If I had I would have said, "Could I have a spear to hold?" But because I didn't think that I would be an actor in my life, I just said I am a leading actor. Why not? So I played a star part the first time I ever walked on a stage, and I have been working my way down ever since.

(Laughter)

FROST: What memories do you have of that radio program that had such a great impact?

WELLES: You mean the scandal?

FROST: Yes. *The War of the Worlds.* That was what year?

WELLES: I know no dates. Just after the invention of the electric light, I know that. I have memories of it. The thing that confuses it in my mind is that we had our own radio show with actors and at the same time we had our own theater, the Mercury Theatre. And the night after the program had an opening on Broadway. So when the police came into the control room and traffic stopped and the world came to an end, we were all saying, "Yes, but have you got the light cue for the second act right?" It didn't quite penetrate until the play had opened that I'd replaced Benedict Arnold as an American villain, and that was because the newspapers, who'd been griping about radio taking away the advertising, finally found somebody to blame. Then they found out that everybody was laughing and thought it was a joke, so in a few days I was suddenly a great fellow, and that's how I got a sponsor.

FROST: What was the part of *The War of the Worlds* that really terrified people?

WELLES: I don't know. Many things, probably. We had an actor who did Roosevelt's voice terribly well, and we brought him on to assure everybody that there was no cause for alarm. I think that's when they really ran out on the streets. We also had a ham radio voice that would come in, identifying himself and trying to talk to other people while this awful thing was happening. We established him, and then we went to a CBS announcer who was describing the arrival of the Martians. And then the announcer began to cough; he couldn't go on and stopped, and then this dead silence. The real trick we did was to hold dead silence on a full network, with no sound at all, and then you'd hear the microphone drop, and then more silence, and then this one little voice, the amateur radio operator, saying, "This is such-and-such. Is there any—" And that is, I guess, when they put the towels on their heads and ran out.

I don't know why they put towels on their heads, but they did. I don't know what they thought that was going to do. A sort of anti-Martian thing.

Then there were all these traffic cops. It was Sunday night and all these guys out in Jersey on their motorcycles waiting, and the people in the cars, driving, had the radio, but the cops didn't. Suddenly everybody started driving at 125 miles an hour. "Pull over!" "No, I'm going to the hills!"

FROST: And if you wanted to terrify people today, how would you do it?

WELLES: I don't. I didn't want to then.

FROST: No, of course. But if somebody wanted to terrify people today, how should they do it?

WELLES: Well, I would say unlimited air time to Spiro Agnew.

(*Laughter*)

FROST: What are your memories now of the making of *Citizen Kane*?

WELLES: Well, of course we had the big scandal, because there was a ridiculous notion that it was based on certain elements in the life of William Randolph Hearst. In those days he owned about seven million newspapers and there was quite a battle. It looked for a while as though they were going to burn the negative and nobody would see it. And that, of course, is the outstanding memory, just getting it on.

FROST: Where did they get that impression from?

WELLES: I can't imagine.

FROST: Funny, isn't it, how people get mistaken ideas. What did inspire you to make *Citizen Kane*?

WELLES: Well, I'll tell you how it started. Inspired seems to be the word. It began with an idea that was used years later in a Japanese film called *Rashomon*, which is several different people telling a story, and you see the same story again, and each time it's different. That was the beginning of *Kane*, but then as the script developed there was just a residue of that idea. There are still elements, but that's how it began.

The main character had to be a person of enormous importance and power. Now, in an open society like ours, except for somebody in politics, who else has such power? Of course, we also had Kane trying to get into politics and unable to make it.

Funny thing about the reactions to that. For a long time *Citizen Kane* was banned in all Communist countries as showing too much of life of a capitalist hyena. At the same time there was a big effort in America to ban it because it was a Communist movie. That left us a rather small public.

FROST: If one looks at all you've done, do you think there's

28

any common thread through it all? Aren't there some things that you know yourself to be preoccupied with?

WELLES: That's the kind of thing that you can see in somebody else's movies better than in your own. If there's any real validity to a book or film, the creator shouldn't be too self-conscious about that. Probably there are these threads but I would be the last person to know them.

FROST: Do you think you're an optimist in your work and in your life?

WELLES: No, I'm a pessimist, but I'm never cynical. It sounds contradictory but it isn't. I hate cynicism more than anything. It is the bad brother of despair, and that's another great sin. I think you can be a pessimist and not want to give up.

FROST: What's a cynic?

WELLES: He thinks it's no good, it's not worth it. All human effort is useless. To him all human virtue is based on ego. He's the fellow who's too smart for everything. I hate that in anybody.

FROST: A cynic is also a fellow who doesn't believe in anything?

WELLES: Yes. Whose view of life and of human values is a cheap one. He underprices the good things of the world.

FROST: What, most of all, do you believe in? God?

WELLES: I suppose that anybody who does not deny the existence of God must finally admit that he does believe in him.

FROST: You once said you respected both atheists and religious people, but not agnostics.

WELLES: That's right.

FROST: Because an agnostic says he doesn't know and you've got to decide one way or the other?

WELLES: I don't think there's a good way of living in the world unless you are one of the two. You must make the tragic decision that we are totally alone in an indifferent universe. This true atheist belief is a noble and splendid position to take, one requiring great courage and character. Or

29

you must be a religious man. The fellow who doesn't do either is copping out in both directions

FROST: Have you made the decision? To be a religious man?

WELLES: Tune in next week and you will hear Orson Welles on that subject. You know that I hate to hear people talking about God? Unless they have a vocation for talking about it.

FROST: But, on the other hand, you said how important it is to make a decision.

WELLES: But I don't have to inform my listeners and viewers about it. It's not because I don't want to tell you my views, but I think the minute you start on that it borders on preaching, and I'm very allergic to that.

I'm also embarrassed by expressions of religion in the movies. I hate it when people pray on the screen. It's not because I hate praying, but whenever I see an actor fold his hands and look up in the spotlight, I'm lost. There's only one other thing in the movies I hate as much, and that's sex. You just can't get in bed or pray to God and convince me on the screen.

FROST: I hesitate to draw any conclusions from that, but is it an indication of the limitations of movies? Loving and praying are two of the most important things in the world. Why can't you do them in the movies?

WELLES: Because they are both conditions of ecstasy, and I think they cannot be communicated unless it's actually happening, in which case the act belongs in a monastery or in a bordello. Ecstasy is really not part of the scene we can do on celluloid.

FROST: Can you do your passion for politics in movies?

WELLES: Any passion, including love. I'm just talking about the act of love.

FROST: Someone said that your films are studies of men in their various conditions, but that there doesn't seem to be enough in them about loving. Do you think that's true?

WELLES: I think it's true, and it's too bad that it's true,

but I don't think it's a fair criticism.' Tne truth is that I've made so many fewer movies than I've wanted to in my life. If I'd made more I'm sure some of them would have included that subject, and now that you've told me about it we'll try and arrange it.

FROST: What is your definition of love?

WELLES: I wish I had a good one. Probably something somebody else said.

FROST: I think Erich Segal, who wrote *Love Story*, said "Love means not feeling you've got to say sorry," and Richard Burton said, "Love means an extraordinary degree of tolerance."

WELLES: Oh, no. If you love somebody you love them *for* their faults, not in spite of them.

FROST: I think that's what he was trying to say. That love is all-embracing. What makes a woman beautiful to you?

WELLES: Human dignity, without which nobody can be beautiful. Women are clearly a superior sex, you know. I really mean that. I'm not trying to make a funny remark or sound smart. I really do think they're much smarter than we are.

FROST: Why?

WELLES: If there hadn't been women we'd still be squatting in a cave eating raw meat, because we made civilization in order to impress our girl friends. And they tolerated it and let us go ahead and play with our toys. We're on one of them now.

FROST: How are they superior?

WELLES: If you don't know that, David, nobody will ever be able to tell you. That's a copout, I know, but—

FROST: I disagree with you. I think they're wonderful and different, but not superior.

WELLES: When I was your age that was my opinion.

FROST: What changed your mind?

WELLES: The passage of the years and the evidence of my senses and of my observation.

FROST: But what did you observe that convinced you?

31

WELLES: No matter what the Bible says—and I'm not a fundamentalist—I just don't think that men were the first. I don't think that Eve was made out of Adam's rib. I think the first sex, biologically, is the female sex, and there are many creatures in our world who are female and only become male as long as is necessary and then revert to the original and superior condition. I think we're a kind of desperation. We're sort of a maddening luxury. The basic and essential human is the woman, and all that we're doing is trying to brighten up the place. That's why all the birds who belong to our sex have prettier feathers—because males have got to try and justify their existence. Look how little we do to keep the race going.

FROST: I find that absolutely fascinating, and I don't agree with a word of it.

WELLES: And I don't blame you.

(*Applause*)

Will God Talk Back to a Playwright?

◆

Tennessee Williams

FROST: A lot of your life has changed since you converted to Roman Catholicism, hasn't it?

WILLIAMS: Oh, yes. That was while I was around the bend. Not that I don't love the Church, I do. I love the Church very much, but I don't go to it. I work, instead.

FROST: But you did convert to Roman Catholicism?

WILLIAMS: Yes, I did.

FROST: Have you stopped that now?

WILLIAMS: It's hard to say. The Church can be so beautiful to look at, you know. I like to go in at odd hours, so none of the congregation is there. I like to go in when it's empty and just kneel down and sort of communicate with whatever there is to communicate with. I hope there is something.

FROST: Do you think there is something?

WILLIAMS: Yes, I do, strangely enough.

FROST: Do you call him God?

WILLIAMS: What other word is there? Godot, I suppose.

FROST: Not that a human being can define God if he is God, but what do you understand by God?

WILLIAMS: Whoever is responsible for the universe. Including us, you know.

FROST: Do you know anything about him? I mean, what is whoever is responsible for the universe like?

WILLIAMS: I think he has odd moments of compassion. I know that every time I have a play opening I will go into

33

a room alone and kneel down and pray, and sometimes it's just a bathroom and I'll kneel down by the bathtub and I'll pray, and I always get a sort of affirmative or negative answer, meaning the show will go or it won't go, you know?

FROST: So you know before it goes on.

WILLIAMS: Not until after I've prayed.

FROST: But after you've prayed, and before it's opened, you know how it's going to do?

WILLIAMS: I get a sort of response, yes.

FROST: And when you say he is responsible for us and for the world, where does his responsibility leave off?

WILLIAMS: Oh, I don't think he's up in the sky or anything like that, you know. Where does our responsibility begin?

FROST: Yes.

WILLIAMS: With ourselves. We have to take that responsibility, it's a terrible one, but we have to assume it.

FROST: And what is the responsibility we have, each of us to ourselves, do you think?

WILLIAMS: We have to see that we are behaving in some sort of a decent fashion toward our fellow creatures, animal and human, don't you think?

FROST: I think particularly human, yes.

WILLIAMS: Particularly human, but animals, too.

FROST: Your plays are full of people with terrible problems and afflictions and so on; do you see life basically as a joyous thing or as a painful thing?

WILLIAMS: I find life quite pleasurable, even though I am insomniac. For instance, I don't sleep until about six in the morning, generally. But I enjoy those hours. I love reading and I even love just lying there and thinking.

FROST: Do you think your plays are basically gloomy?

WILLIAMS: People tell me they are, but I've never thought so.

FROST: Which would you say was the most hopeful play you've written?

34

WILLIAMS: Certainly *Period of Adjustment*. It is the only comedy I ever wrote, but then I saw it again and I suddenly realized it was not funny. There were laughs in it, but it was really more serious than I had thought. It had another title, which was a better title, actually, *Hi-Point Over a Cabin*. It was laid in the suburbs of a city and the suburb was named Hi-Point. My mother's house is built over an underground cavern. She discovered that after she'd bought it and moved in it began to sink little by little, and cracks appeared in the wall and the ceilings.

FROST: Has your own life influenced all that you've written a great deal? People say they can see you in your plays.

WILLIAMS: I'm very personal as a writer, yes. I don't mean to be, I just am. Unavoidably.

FROST: Which is the most personal of your plays?

WILLIAMS: Perhaps *Camino Real*.

FROST: Why do you pick that?

WILLIAMS: It was sort of a statement of my own philosophy, a credo.

FROST: What is your credo?

WILLIAMS: That romanticism is absolutely essential. That we can't really live bearably without a good deal of it. It's very painful, but we need it.

FROST: By romanticism do you mean fantasy?

WILLIAMS: A certain amount of that and the ability to feel tenderness toward another human being. The ability to love.

FROST: And what gives people that ability?

WILLIAMS: Not allowing themselves to become brutalized by the brutalizing experiences that we do encounter on the Camino Real.

FROST: How would you define the word "love"?

WILLIAMS: Love is a feeling, isn't it?

FROST: What sort?

WILLAMS: Oh, well, there's sexual love. The first time I felt that, I was really just a child of eleven. I had a child-

35

hood sweetheart. I was sitting next to her in a moving picture theater called the Lyric—the West End Lyric in St. Louis, and she was a redheaded girl with brown eyes and she had no sleeves on her dress and I wanted to put my arm around her and feel her bare arm, and that was my first awakening of sexual love. Later I began to feel great tenderness toward her of a nonsexual nature.

FROST: What sort of love would you call that, as opposed to sexual love?

WILLIAMS: We'd call that the purification. Wouldn't you? I think that sexual love is usually the best introduction to love, but I do think there is something beyond it, just as I know that people at very advanced ages still feel great love for each other.

FROST: It doesn't necessarily replace sexual love, but goes beyond it?

WILLIAMS: Sometimes it even replaces it. In cases of couples who are married for fifty or sixty years, I don't suppose they still want to have sexual relations. I shouldn't imagine so, although it's possible, they tell me.

FROST: I heard they go on forever.

WILLIAMS: Oh, really? That's encouraging.

FROST: But you mentioned experiencing the first sexual love feelings at the age of eleven. How often have you felt that purification of love, how often have you gone beyond that?

WILLIAMS: I've never enumerated the times. I've never lived without feeling love, though.

FROST: Really?

WILLIAMS: Yes. I'm talking too intimately to you. Let's get on to something more general.

FROST: All right. What was the spur that initially started you writing, do you think?

WILLIAMS: My mother bought me a typewriter when I was thirteen and I think I'd already shown some interest in writing. Probably around eleven, you know, but at thirteen she bought me a typewriter and then I went to business school and became more or less a pro.

FROST: Did the school know you were training to do something artistic like plays?

WILLIAMS: No, they thought I was training to become a clerk-typist, which I did later on.

FROST: For how long?

WILLIAMS: For three years, in the International Shoe Company in St. Louis, and I had to have a nervous breakdown to get out of it.

(*Laughter*)

FROST: How did you manage that?

WILLIAMS: I just had it. You would have, too, if you'd been in that. But I wouldn't take anything for those three years. I got to know those people so well. Otherwise I might have grown up knowing only long-haired artists, writers, and poets. I love them, but that's not the world.

FROST: What was it you learned in those three years that you couldn't learn from artists?

WILLIAMS: These people's lives were rather barren, and their great joy was in communicating with each other and telling every little detail of their daily lives to each other, and bonds were formed. I've never had any similar relationship since, because I've been sort of isolated with the typewriter most of the time.

FROST: Would you say your life has been lonely?

WILLIAMS: No, no. No, I've always found it necessary to have one person, at least one, very close to me. It's awful when the person dies. I've had that experience. At the age of fifty-eight, which is my age, it's natural to have had that experience. And then you have to start building a new world.

FROST: Is that difficult?

WILLIAMS: Or else you drink yourself blind or something like that. Or retreat into some false world of liquor, pills, or drugs, or what have you.

FROST: You were, thank God, cured recently.

37

WILLIAMS: Yes, they gave me the cold-turkey treatment and I had three convulsions in one morning. I don't know how I survived it, but I did.

FROST: You survived it and you look incredibly well now. You really were quite close to death. Does death frighten you?

WILLIAMS: Not nearly as much, not nearly. There was one moment in this psychiatric hospital when I had a heart attack and I felt the stabbing pains. What I felt wasn't fear, but a sort of a cold concentration on the moment. There happened to be a sadistic nurse in the room. She had followed me in because I had gone out of the room very angry and said that there was too much disturbance and I couldn't sleep and all that. She had followed me into my little cubicle. It wasn't a plush hospital at all, it was sort of a snake pit with almost no refinements. And she had followed me into this cell and she said, "Well, what's next on the agenda?" And I turned to her and I said, "You're a mean little bitch." And then, all of a sudden I began having these stabbing pains and I said, "Go get me a nitroglycerin tablet."

FROST: And did she go and get it?

WILLIAMS: She did. So it shows that they're never really that mean.

FROST: You say that you're not lonely. Would you say that you're a happy person?

WILLIAMS: I think so. Relatively. I try not to feel sorry for myself.

FROST: What is being happy, really?

WILLIAMS: I don't know. Does anyone? I think that the greatest happiness is felt in moments of great tenderness between two people. Isn't that about as much as we know?

FROST: Is it that any one person yearns to communicate with another and it's only in those moments of love that they can most deeply communicate? Why are those the peaks of happiness?

WILLIAMS: Because we all have a great desire to escape

from ourselves and to feel joined to another human being.

FROST: Why do we like to escape from ourselves?

WILLIAMS: Because to be alone is to be lonely. Unless you're a writer and you have your typewriter.

FROST: Do you like yourself or not? Or do you adore yourself?

WILLIAMS: I don't adore myself, no.

FROST: Do you find yourself good company?

WILLIAMS: I never stopped to think about that very much. I'm more or less saddled with myself. I can't do much about it. Do I like myself? No, I don't like myself very much. I often wonder, how can anybody like me, and yet occasionally I discover that somebody does.

FROST: Given that you're not lonely and that basically you try to be happy, why is it that your plays are so full of the less cheerful topics, like cancer and lobotomies and rape and adultery and incest and nymphomania and homosexuality and—

WILLIAMS: You're merely picking things out of the plays.

FROST: Nevertheless, the abiding impression that people get from reading your plays is of those spectacularly cheerless subjects.

WILLIAMS: Don't you know that those are the things that we are all obliged to live with? You may not die of cancer, and yet eventually you might. So it's a part of human existence, isn't it? I've only dealt with cerebral lobotomy once. In a play called *Suddenly Last Summer*. It was a dramatic necessity.

FROST: What put that subject into your mind?

WILLIAMS: I happened to know about it, not to experience it on my own, but—

FROST: Or through the family?

WILLIAMS: Some person that I had known well that had a cerebral lobotomy.

FROST: It just comes back again and again to the fact that all your plays do come out of your personal life, don't they?

WILLIAMS: Out of everybody's personal life. I think we

all live with rape. My God, we're all victims of rape, symbolically.

FROST: How?

WILLIAMS: Society rapes the individual.

FROST: Do we all live with cannibalism in this same symbolic way?

WILLIAMS: Yes, we all devour each other, in our fashion.

FROST: What about things like the homosexuality and so on, does everybody live with that, too?

WILLIAMS: I think that everybody has some elements of homosexuality in him, even the most heterosexual of us.

FROST: That no one is all man or all woman, you mean?

WILLIAMS: Oh, in my experience, no. I don't want to be involved in some sort of a scandal, but I've covered the waterfront.

(*Laughter and applause*)

What Kind of Lip Do You Expect from a Trumpeter?

◆

Louis Armstrong

FROST: Louis, how many records have you made?

ARMSTRONG: It's hard for me to count them, because all I wanted to do is make that scene there, and let the man slip that green in my hand, so I could go uptown and have a ball.

FROST: Two thousand five hundred, somebody told me you've recorded.

ARMSTRONG: Yeah, quite a few. I have them all, you know. I put them all on tape to make sure I have them. Priceless, way back there, you know. That same horn, like when I used to play behind Bessie Smith.

FROST: When did you first play an instrument? That was in New Orleans, wasn't it?

ARMSTRONG: Well, I was in the boys' waif home. Colored Waif Home for Boys, that was the name of the orphanage. And I used to follow behind King Oliver in the parades. And quite naturally I went over to do some shooting with my stepfather, celebrating New Year's Eve, you know.

See, around New Year's Eve everybody . . . celebrate with it, you know. So I found this pistol that had blanks in it. But the noise, everybody gets it. So when I look around, the old guy was shooting a little old six shooter across the street there. Bang, bang, bang, bang. So I was singing . . . we used to go around and pass the hat, you know. And they called me Dipper at that time, Dippermouth, you know. They said, "Get him, Dipper." And took it out and, bang, bang, bang, straightened it up, until that detective was hug-

41

ging me. "You can celebrate all you want if they don't get you."

So the little bugle boy went home. So they gave me the bugle, and had me to learn the calls, you know, taps, and when they go to bed, and mess calls. That was my favorite one, that mess call, you know. And I used to be devilish, and I'd hold it up some time. And, oh, those cats said, "Man, if you don't blow that call!"

So finally a little kid in the band went home, so they gave me the cornet. And they taught me *Home Sweet Home*, and different things. And Mr. Peter Davis, who had the band, you know, two keepers, one who teachers the music, and they had one that teached the kids carpentry and different things, Mr. Alexander. And Mr. Jones, he just come out to tend cavalry, the head man, teached them how to drill with wooden guns, and everything.

I was ready with the first war, because I knew all about "shoulder arms" and "parade rest," and, you know, "retreat," and all that stuff.

But anyway, they put me in the little band, and in a month's time they made me leader of the little old band. So I learned a lot.

FROST: How old were you?

ARMSTRONG: Thirteen years old; you see, I stayed there till I was fourteen. And during that time the little band used to go into the city and play, and pass the hat around.

FROST: That was a fantastic area for a young chap, because there was the red-light district—

ARMSTRONG: Red-light district, and everything.

FROST: Storyville, and so on. What are your memories of that?

ARMSTRONG: We wasn't allowed in the red-light district. But boys thirteen years old, you know what I mean, that sun down on them all the time, they looked like old men anyhow. So all we had to do was put on long pants, they wouldn't know the difference. That's how I got to hear Manny Perez, all the best bands, and everything.

FROST: They were all in the red-light district.

ARMSTRONG: Yeah. Each corner had a band. Cabarets, they called them. And the honkytonks later, that's where I played, in my neighborhood, where all the bad guys and the—what do you call—those girls up the street, I don't know.

(*Laughter*)

But they liked me, because I was young all right, but they liked the way I played the blues. And so I never got in trouble. And they protected me. And guys got to shooting in every cabaret there.

FROST: There was real shooting?

ARMSTRONG: Oh, yes. Man, you'd think they was cowboys and Indians. Every Sunday morning, get behind posts, boom, shooting and trying to get one another, you know.

FROST: Why did they do it on Sunday morning?

ARMSTRONG: Well, they'd been up all night gambling, and the girls working, and everything, and everybody stoned. Be like they get their revenge before they go home.

FROST: Is that a good atmosphere for a musician?

ARMSTRONG: I thought it was lovely.

(*Laughter and applause*)

And, you know, I loved those people because they never did tell me nothing wrong about life, you know what I mean.

FROST: What did they tell you?

ARMSTRONG: Well, I mean, for instance, the toughest guy in the honkytonk that runs the gambling, you know, in the back room—he knew I was getting ready to come up North, and I was going to play with King Oliver, and so forth. And this pep talk he give me said, "Look here, son, I like the way you blow that quail." That was my cornet, I knew what he was talking about. "Now, you go up North, and always have a white man behind you to say, 'That's my nigger.'" And I swear he playing with me. Now you can figure that out yourself. That was the talk.

And Joe Grady came right in to see, and it was just like that. Because he knew I wanted to blow my horn, and he saw to that. I didn't worry about getting in battles. And Joe knew that if I didn't find him, I was going to go back. Because I knew they loved the way I played my horn in that honkytonk.

FROST: And what the guy was saying, giving you the advice, was that—

ARMSTRONG: That's the love he had for me. "You go up there and blow that horn, because I like the way you blow it. And everybody else better like it." That's the way he gave it to me. You understand? Even when I was in the orphanage in this little band, and worked around my neighborhood, all them same old gamblers and hustlers, they asked Mr. Davis, the leader, "Say, can we pick up some money to put in Louis Armstrong's cap?" He said, "Yes, all right." So they filled my cap with dollars, and nickels, quarters, everything. So when I got back to the orphanage and counted that money, we had enough money to buy brand-new instruments for the whole band.

FROST: What else would you say you learned about life in those days?

ARMSTRONG: Everything, everything. Like from the rudimentals, because I didn't steal much. But the nicest things, in their ways, might sound crude. I could see the wrong in this guy, you take some, you leave some. That's the way it works. And that's my life.

FROST: Take some, leave some.

ARMSTRONG: You know what I mean, the good and the bad, different things like that. Well, I ain't going to follow this guy if I know he's wrong. Tried that in the orphanage, you know, trying to be a big shot with the kids. And I knew I had no business with a pistol, but all the rest of the kids had pistols, so why shouldn't I have one?

FROST: Right, but you—

ARMSTRONG: I didn't run with those boys, I wouldn't have even thought about it.

FROST: But you were the one that got caught.

ARMSTRONG: And they followed the leader, and crazy

44

things like that. You got bad boys that go in a grocery store, and you just going in there with them. But when you look around and see he got a whole ham under his coat, now you got to run too, you know. That's what I mean, the environment. And finally I got away from all that.

FROST: Louis, we were talking earlier on about the guy who loved you enough to say, "That's my nigger."

ARMSTRONG: Well, in those days, I mean—

FROST: It didn't hurt your feelings?

ARMSTRONG: I was raised up with them people. That's the only way they could explain themselves. They wasn't the most intelligent people, but they all good hearts, you know what I mean? And they don't harm nobody. They don't take nothing from nobody, or take nothing off anybody.

And when they give you a pep talk like that, that's love, you understand? Like the gals used to call me, you know, in the honkytonks, and maybe they're pimps and they're gambling, and so forth. Well, I'm blowing them blues, and they all like the way I'm blowing, and they come in with their stockings full of money, and everything like that, and they love me so much. And every now and then one of them make me sit on their lap, you know what I mean, and have a bottle of beer. I say, "Don't you think I better get up now?" "Get up from there, boy!" And that's all. They loved me.

FROST: You said at one point that you took your first professional engagement because you'd started hanging out with the pretty chicks and you needed operating money. Can you remember meeting the first chick you thought was pretty?

ARMSTRONG: You're asking an awful lot there. (*Laughter*)
Boy, what a memory you have. Well, I don't know, but I met some nice people in my day.

FROST: You're a great expert, though, in making women happy. What's the secret of making women happy? (*Laughter*)

ARMSTRONG: Well, I don't know, I did all right, I had four wives. I did all right. Didn't any of them try to hurt me. When we separated we remained the best of friends. And the ones that's here on earth today, still good friends.

There's Lucille, which is my fourth wife. And there's Lil, who's living in Chicago now, was my second wife. And they're good friends. And they go out and have lunch, when they meet. And going down the street together, you know, walking, and a bunch of cats would say, "Hey, Mrs. Armstrong," and both of them would turn around. (*Laughter*)

I had a beautiful life with all my wives, yeah. One is, like I say, in Chicago, you know. Every time we got a divorce, no alimony or nothing, we straightened that deal, boom, right there. Whatever success I had with that wife, it's all hers. And I started all over again. That's right.

FROST: That's great, and it's tidy.

ARMSTRONG: It's better. I didn't go for that alimony, you know, catch you when you can, and every time you look around they lock you up, and no way to settle this. "Let's settle this right now, baby," you know. And we sign, and that's it. That's why we're still the best of friends. Now if she go and throw it away, that's her business, you know what I mean. But I ain't never paid alimony yet, and I don't think I will now, because Lucille got four stars, and like, man, she's got it all tied up.

FROST: But you've been married to Lucille for how long?

ARMSTRONG: It's going on to twenty-eight or twenty-nine years. That's a long time.

Ain't no use either one of us thinking about going to that road again, you know, getting married, and all that. We had so long to get the right understanding there, so we don't have to bother about nothing now. That's it.

46

What Kind of Universal Language Is More Popular Than Esperanto?

◆

Mr. and Mrs. Artur Rubinstein

FROST: You've been described many times as the finest classical pianist in the history of the world. And do you know, not only have you got fantastic hands, but you've got the most expressive face in the world.

RUBINSTEIN: Well, they tell me always that I make faces, you know. I was told that by somebody some time in South Africa when I tried to get diamonds for my wife rather cheaper from the South African mogul, Oppenheimer, who owns De Beers Diamond Society, and I couldn't meet him easily there. He was always somewhere else.

But at a concert in Johannesburg, his wife arrived covered with jewels, and she came backstage and said, "Oh, I heard so much about you from the Duke of Devonshire, who traveled with me on the boat." You know, he was then Under Secretary of—

FROST: One of those things.

RUBINSTEIN: Something, yes. We played bridge together on the boat. She said, "Ah, he talked so much about you, and may I ask you a favor?" Oh, I thought, she will ask me to play the Tchaikowsky Concerto as an encore or something like that. I said, "Anything, of course, if I can, anything." She said, "Would you make some faces? Because the Duke of Devonshire said to me, 'This fellow makes such faces like nobody in the world, you know.'"

So, that impressed me a little bit. Now I try not to make faces any more.

47

FROST: Oh, don't stop. Don't ever stop.

RUBINSTEIN: I did make some faces because I'm now, if you don't know it yet, the great coming film star.

FROST: Ah, because of the film of your life. Called *The Love of Life*.

RUBINSTEIN: It was shown in Paris for four months to crowds, if you please. I don't brag now. I'm just telling you the simple truth. And it went to Hollywood and it was nominated.

FROST: Love of life actually is what your life's been all about, hasn't it?

RUBINSTEIN: Yes, it's called *Love of Life* because you see I do love life tremendously. That is my philosophy, which I won on a day when I wanted to commit suicide. That's very strange, but it's true. You see, I was on zero. A young man of twenty always reaches somehow the bottom one way or another. Despair about love affair or no money or your parents, school or something, you know.

In my case it was everything. I didn't have enough success. I had absolutely no money. I was in love with a lady who didn't—well, it didn't go very well, you know. I was all alone, and I didn't want anybody to know it.

And so I decided to die. Well, I didn't.

FROST: What went wrong?

RUBINSTEIN: How I tried to do it?

FROST: Yes.

RUBINSTEIN: I was alone in a hotel in Berlin, nobody knew where I was, you see. One day I was absolutely at the bottom. I had nothing. They wanted to throw me out of the hotel. I couldn't pay my bill. So I wanted to hang myself there in the bathroom on a sort of bathrobe belt, but it was very tired, very tired. So, when I put it on, I fell on the floor.

Well, I cried a little. I was a bit hysterical about it. Then when I walked out into the street, I suddenly discovered happiness, you know, love of life, because I saw what a damned fool I was, excuse the expression. Everything is at my dis-

48

position, even in a hospital or in prison or anywhere, on a deathbed.

If you feel inside happiness, I needed only to think of music or look at beautiful women around or flowers or think about something beautiful or take a good book into my hands. Nothing mattered. And that prevailed ever since. I am probably the happiest man I have ever met.

FROST: And you really, then, lived life to the full. You said that you never rehearsed as much when you were young as you should because of wine, women, and song, as it were.

RUBINSTEIN: I loved life so much. I was so frightfully concerned about everything, you see. I wanted to know everything, see everything. I didn't want to miss anything. So, I hated to be a slave of the keyboard. For me, the keyboard and to play scales was like brushing the teeth. (*Gargles a scale*) I couldn't stand it. I never did it.

Well, of course, I was born with good fingers. I mean fingers also are born, you know, not only the talent for music, but you must be born with the right fingers.

FROST: Well now, what specially—

RUBINSTEIN: Well, I'll show you. Practically everybody has a very small last finger, but mine is almost as long as the next one.

FROST: I see, yes.

RUBINSTEIN: I have a small hand, but I have a huge stretch. I can grab a lot of notes on the piano. It helps. There's a lot of things that help too.

And above all, you know what helps? Good luck. That's a very important thing.

FROST: What sort of good luck did you have?

RUBINSTEIN: Good luck means that I lived always with miracles, and things came to me. I was dreaming to do this. It came toward me, you know. And I believe now in a very strange philosophy. If you love life as much as I do, life loves you, too.

Grouchy people, those who are always dissatisfied, saying, "Grrr, I am sick, and I am not happy, I have no money . . ."

49

well, it gets worse and worse, you know. They are never satisfied. They are always complaining. "The last one, I lost all the money on the Wall Street." They always come with something worse.

But the people who love life, somehow things happen. Things happen in the right way. And it did in my life, all the time. I met the right wife, right there. She's sitting there.

FROST: Let's introduce you, yes, please. (*Applause*) Come and join us.

MRS. RUBINSTEIN: How do you do?

RUBINSTEIN: You see, I must tell you that the idea for the film, most ideas for the film came from her.

MRS. RUBINSTEIN: Yes, well, I always wanted to have some sort of record, you know. I thought it's a crime in our time and age not to have any record of a man like my husband, whom I adore, and I think he was worthy of something to be left outside of just records. And it just happened, the whole thing happened more or less like a tryout, a joke or something, and then it grew into very important proportions, and I'm quite happy about it.

FROST: How long have you both been married?

MRS. RUBINSTEIN: Better not ask.

RUBINSTEIN: Shall we tell him?

MRS. RUBINSTEIN: Yes.

RUBINSTEIN: Thirty-seven years.

FROST: And how old are you now, Artur?

RUBINSTEIN: Eighty-three.

FROST: How do you keep him so young?

MRS. RUBINSTEIN: I don't keep him young. He keeps me young. That's true. I can hardly follow his pace. It's tremendous.

RUBINSTEIN: It's funny, really. I don't feel my age at all, you know. I never change my life since about forty, fifty years. I never lie down in the afternoon or never take any pills. I do all the silly things, I always did, you know, I can go to two movies. I can watch your things here on television until three in the morning.

FROST: Tell me, do audiences vary in different parts of

50

the world? Is it the same reaction, the same yells and applause wherever you go, or is it different?

RUBINSTEIN: Well, different, *attentieuse* and so on, but I must say the public in general responds the same way. There isn't such a thing as what do the Japanese do about this or that. No. The same pieces have more or less the same impact on the public. If I please with a piece in Cincinnati, I know I can please with the same piece in Moscow or in Tokyo or in anywhere. There is an appeal, it must be human appeal, there is a secret language of music which just does that with a human being. It ought to, in any case. If it doesn't, then it's my fault.

But music by Bach, by Beethoven, by Mozart, by Schubert, by Chopin, ought to get into the hearts of everybody, and I remark that it can do that.

FROST: When you say get into the hearts, what's the most emotional piece of music you play?

RUBINSTEIN: Ah, don't ask me about any sort of champion in anything. This is a question which is impossible for us to answer. There isn't such a thing as a best piece.

FROST: No, but is there a piece that moves you more than any other?

RUBINSTEIN: No, no, no. You know, the minute I would feel that way, all the other pieces would have a second rank, you know. It's impossible. Whatever I play is the piece, and there is no other one at the moment I play it.

FROST: Is there a piece of Artur's that you prefer more than any other?

MRS. RUBINSTEIN: Well, I must say the same thing. He moves me, sometimes less, sometimes more, but it depends on him, on his disposition, on the piano, on the sound, and I also vary. I don't always respond to the same, let's say, nocturne of Chopin or something, no. I can cry, there are certain musics, certain things that I react to physically practically. There are certain things of Schumann, for instance, a phrase or just a few bars, and I start crying. I don't know why, I just can't resist that. Happens with Chopin.

RUBINSTEIN: But not always. You know, everything is a

world, per se, in itself. If I ask you which is the painter you prefer, Rembrandt, Velázquez, Titian, Leonardo da Vinci, Goya. If you know that there is a big exhibition of each one of those which I mentioned, you will run and forget that there are any others.

FROST: Right.

RUBINSTEIN: Then it isn't a thing of the best pianist, the best violinist, the best conductor. All this is sheer nonsense. In practice, there isn't such a thing as the best. It's simply a different one.

FROST: You don't think you're the best at anything?

RUBINSTEIN: No, I wouldn't say it, no, no, no, no. I'm a pianist who appeals to a lot of publics, and I'm very happy about that. But I know that if another pianist is wonderful, he will also appeal to them in another way, just as I told you about the painters. It doesn't mean anything when they write, "He's the best, the greatest violinist," that is nonsense. There isn't the greatest composer. They are all different, you see.

FROST: There is such a thing as genius, isn't there?

RUBINSTEIN: Of course, the creators are geniuses. We are small talents.

FROST: But you don't think the interpretive genius—

RUBINSTEIN: We are talents. We are interpreters. I would say proudly we are a little bit like painters. You see, a creator of music is like God, really, because he creates music from nowhere and it fills your heart.

Painters, sculptors, and so on speak in third person. They describe something. They show you something. It's not the same thing. They show you a landscape. They show you a portrait of a lady or a still-life. They show you a fruit dish or an apple or something. Even abstracts have to show you something. They show you colors. They show you combination, construction, you see what I mean?

FROST: Absolutely.

RUBINSTEIN: Well, we pianists, I mean interpreters in general, we are given to play a Beethoven sonata. A Beethoven sonata talks to us like a landscape talks to a painter or a face talks to a painter. So, it talks differently to each pianist who looks at the same sonata. Just as if you were painted by those painters I mentioned, they would paint you all with the conviction that you can't be painted otherwise, but you would be different in each picture.

FROST: And when you hear other pianists play something, some great piece of music, you can see it is completely different from the way you—

RUBINSTEIN: Of course. And I'm vastly interested. I forget that I play the same piece.

FROST: Do you get very nervous before a performance?

RUBINSTEIN: Yes, very. And I think it's a necessity. If you are not nervous, there is something indifferent about the performance. Mostly I'm very, very nervous. Not frightened of the public. There are two kinds of nervousnesses. There's one where you have trembling legs, you lose your memory, and if I see that in a young pupil, I say, "You will never, never, never play in public." But there is that other nervousness, called *trac* in French. It's . . . what is it? There's another word for it.

MRS. RUBINSTEIN: Stage fright. You see, I came in handy.

RUBINSTEIN: Lovely. Thank you. You see, there is the feeling of concentration, right? I feel myself always a little bit like a racehorse, having to do the best, you know.

The horrible thing in our life is that we must be for the public at least, for their money, perfect at eight-thirty, not tomorrow morning. I couldn't say to the public, "Well, look here, I'm not now in the mood. I'm a little bit tired. Come back in about two hours or tomorrow morning." So, we must face it. Sometimes we have a headache, we receive a telegram, we have bad news. Suddenly you feel something in your arm or a pain or something. They don't care. And if you tell them that something is wrong, you can play like God Almighty, they will always say, "Poor fellow, one heard that he was sick with a pain or something."

Famous singers, you know, are always very nervous. They send out the manager, who says, "Mr. Spaghettini is a little

53

bit indisposed tonight, and so we ask your sympathy for that," and he comes out suddenly he feels great, and he sings the best. The public says, "Poor Spaghettini." They're so sorry for him. Very dangerous.

FROST: Have you ever done a performance with an injured finger, for instance?

RUBINSTEIN: Listen, I played in Los Angeles two concerts with a small finger which burst open. I had a bad piano, deaf piano, dumb piano, in Denver, Colorado, on the way to Los Angeles, and yet I wanted to give my best all the same, you see, so I was playing with such terrific effort that the small finger burst open, and that hurt me dreadfully. I arrived in Los Angeles with despair. And I had a concert the next day.

They gave me something, by a drugstore they gave me a fantastic little vitamin. . . . They made me smear it up every twenty minutes. The next morning I was all right—wonderful, really.

FROST: So, you'd recommend it to all pianists injured in Denver, Colorado?

RUBINSTEIN: Well, I would.

FROST: Do you have good-luck charms and things like that?

RUBINSTEIN: Yes. I am very superstitious. In every country, in every city, they give me another superstition. I remember once a bearded Russian who was the electrician of Diaghilev's ballet. And Diaghilev was always penniless, couldn't pay his company. He was too lavish, too luxurious, so the whole production was always so expensive.

So, this electrician in Barcelona, in Spain, phone me up, "Could you lend me some money?"

I liked the man, so I said, "Yes, come up to my room, and I will let you have it."

I waited for him, he knocked at the door, he opened it and he said, "Aagh!" and ran away.

You know, a man who asks you for money and runs away is a very extraordinary creature. I ran after him to find out what was what. I was scared, you know, I thought there was some animal in my room. I said, "What happened?" you see.

"The hat. The hat."

I said, "What?"

He saw my hat on the bed.

MRS. RUBINSTEIN: That's bad luck, but he didn't know it until then.

RUBINSTEIN: That death is coming when you throw your hat on a bed. Well, you know very well that since that I never put my hat on a bed.

How Does It Feel to Be a First Lady Longer Than Eleanor Roosevelt?

◆

Helen Hayes

FROST: Miss Hayes, when did you first become aware of being the proud possessor of the title "First Lady of the American Stage"?

HAYES: Well, that was a little distressing. Do you really want me to tell the truth?

FROST: Yes.

HAYES: I had a radio show of my own, way, way back when there was no television. And on the dress rehearsal I heard the announcer referring to me as the First Lady of the American Stage. And I was so frightened by this, I rushed back to the control booth and said, "You can't say that. A lot of people call Katherine Cornell the first lady."

And my agent grabbed me and said, "Keep quiet, they have to have something special to sell you with, and they've made up that title for you." So I was made the First Lady of the American Stage by General Foods.

(*Laughter and applause*)

Isn't it awful!

FROST: When was that?

HAYES: Back in the thirties or forties, I think. Yes, late thirties, early forties.

FROST: Who would you pick today as the first gentleman of the American stage?

HAYES: Of course, Alfred Lunt immediately comes to mind, but of the more active people, I think this wonderful Dustin Hoffman is fast becoming something. It's terrible,

56

though, to choose a name, isn't it, because you'll forget the most important.

FROST: Well, it's off the top of your head, so that's all right. When anybody says, "Why didn't you pick me?" you can say, "Oh, I just forgot you for a second." But I'd love to see Dustin Hoffman and you costar together.

HAYES: Yes, I could play his great-grandmamma, or something like that.

FROST: The part you've been playing in *The Front Page* was modeled on your mother, right?

HAYES: That's my impression. Charlie, my husband (who wrote the play, of course, with Ben Hecht), never admitted that to me.

FROST: They never actually said it?

HAYES: Oh, no. Charlie was too smart for that. Because she isn't a very sympathetic character. She's a little ridiculous and pompous. I don't think he would have dared tell me that. We weren't married then. He might have told me after.

FROST: Was there one bit that you particularly thought was your husband writing a character like your mother?

HAYES: Well, when Hildy Johnson says to someone, "I've got three tickets on the train for New York. For me, and my girl, and her goddamn ma." And I knew that that was my Charlie writing from his heart.

(*Laughter*)

So it's wonderful to be able to play my mother. I adored her, and still revere her, and remember her as a witty, delightful woman. Though none of that comes out in this portrait of Ben's and Charlie's.

FROST: From what I read, the very success of Charlie's play, *The Front Page*, helped you to get married, didn't it? I gather that he didn't want to marry you until he'd really made it, the same way you had.

HAYES: That's right.

FROST: Tell us about it.

HAYES: Oh, I was a star in a play called *Coquette*, and I was launched on a very successful star career then. I had

57

been starred in two or three others before that, but this was my greatest success up until that time. And Charlie refused to have anything to do with planning a wedding while I was way up there and he was not known too well.

And the opening night of *The Front Page*, the producer of both *Coquette* and *The Front Page*, Jed Harris, closed *Coquette* for the night and let me go to see Charlie's opening. I was such a lovesick girl, nothing mattered to me but that I would get Charlie.

And I sat up in the balcony of that theater and waited to see how it was going to go. And a wonderful actress named Dorothy Stickney came roaring on, played a great scene as Molly Malloy, and roared off. The house cheered. And I knew that I was going to be married.

(*Laughter*)

FROST: That's great. Did you tell Dorothy Stickney what she'd done for you that night?

HAYES: I've never stopped telling her.

FROST: When did your career actually begin? You started really very young. At four or five, wasn't it?

HAYES: Yes, indeed, I was weaned on greasepaint, I think. I was a pupil of Miss Minnie Hawkes' dancing classes in Washington, D.C. And Miss Minnie used to have a little spring festival, to show off our great talent as pupils. I was there to correct a turned-in toe, which never got corrected. I was no particular credit to Miss Minnie as a dancer, because I tripped over that bad toe all the time.

So they devised a little miming number for me to do. I was doing a little song called *The Gibson Bathing Girl*, and striking attitudes of this then very popular figure in American magazines. And that was when I was five, or six, I guess.

FROST: Did you ever get to sing any of the song too? Can you remember any of it?

HAYES: Oh, yes.

FROST: Really?

HAYES: Yes, I'll sing it for you. If you want to be en-

58

couraged about the lyrics of today, just listen to this, from 1906, or whatever it was.

> Why do they call me the Gibson Girl,
> Gibson Girl, Gibson Girl?
> What is the matter with Mr. Ibsen, Mr. Ibsen?
> Why does a Gibson wear a blank expression
> And a monumental curl?
> Walk with a bend in your back,
> And they'll call you the Gibson girl!

Now isn't that brilliant?

FROST: Marvelous. What's the most difficult acting assignment you've ever had?

HAYES: I think the next one is always the most difficult Everything is worse in anticipation, including acting. Opening night. Doing this show with you. I'm so happy now, but I felt terrible when I was coming over here.

FROST: You didn't.

HAYES: I was scared. Oh, yes, yes. Don't you?

FROST: Well, I'm untypical, I think. I never get nervous But it's absolutely fantastic that you still do, because you know everything's going to be a triumph for you.

HAYES: I have news for you. It's going to get worse and worse as you get older and older.

FROST: It is?

HAYES: Yes. I wasn't nervous when I was your age.

FROST: By show nine thousand and twenty I shall be a wreck, shall I?

HAYES: That's right. I'll be standing there to fan you.

FROST: What about *Victoria Regina*? Was that difficult?

HAYES: Oh, it was, undoubtedly. Because it went from the age of seventeen to her diamond jubilee. All those different ages frightened me very much. So much so that—I don't think I've ever told this to anyone before—but I went to England to try to convince the writer of the play, Laurence Housman, that the play really was over with Albert's death, and that there was nothing of any enormous interest after that.

You know, it's a series of vignettes, very short plays. And they were put together into nine scenes. And I said the last three scenes, which constituted the last act, were really a letdown after Albert's death. That was because I didn't want to do them. I was afraid.

If he hadn't been a very stubborn old fellow, about eighty-five years old, I would never have been in this glorious success. A younger, anxious playwright might have been swayed by me, and had cut those last scenes out, and that would have been the end of that.

FROST: He just stuck firm?

HAYES: It was sheer panic that made me do it. Oh, yes. He said, "Don't do my play if you can't do those."

FROST: Did you do a great deal of preparation for the role?

HAYES: Oh, yes. In all of the research I did on Queen Victoria I realized that this was a woman who was not really born with that special genius for ruling, perhaps that Queen Elizabeth I had, and that your Queen Elizabeth II seems to have. She was really a rather middle-class hausfrau, you know.

There she was, thrown into ruling the greatest empire the world has ever known. And for a long time in her career she was not beloved; she was very much scorned and despised by the British people. Because they used to say, "She's so middle-class."

But then of course she lived and reigned long enough to become beloved. You can always get beloved if you can hang around long enough.

(*Laughter*)

Durability is the thing. They're loving me more than they ever loved me twenty years ago, when I was much better than I am now.

FROST: You did Victoria with an accent, didn't you? Is

60

the wretched old English accent a nuisance to have to do right through a play?

HAYES: I—

FROST: I try and keep it up for ninety minutes, you know.

(*Laughter*)

HAYES: I was afraid to try the English accent, because American audiences would think I was putting on, and being la-dee-da. And I was in quite a dilemma. So someone had told me that it was rumored that she had a very faint German accent because her mother was a German.

So I was once allowed to see the Dowager Marchioness of Milfordhaven, who was her granddaughter. I went to call on her in Kensington Palace before I did the play. I said, "Did your grandmother, Her Majesty, have any German accent?" And she said, "Ach, no, she hat no more dan you or me."

(*Laughter*)

What Does a Male Hustler Do for an Encore?

◆

Jon Voight

FROST: Jon, did you always want to be an actor?

VOIGHT: I guess I really did. I didn't know it until I was through college, but at stages all along the way I got involved at some level or another. And then I finally got through school and everyone was hoping I'd do something decent with my life. My father was hoping I'd be a lawyer or something. And I said, "Well, listen, I've played the game long enough. Now I'm going to go and be an actor," and so I did.

FROST: Did you qualify as a lawyer or what?

VOIGHT: Someone told me I had been offered a law scholarship from the university's law school. I don't believe it, because I tend not to believe that I'm really qualified in that area.

FROST: You deliberately don't believe it so you don't have to go and do it?

VOIGHT: Something like that. I think that I'm always able to kind of get by on my personality. People believe what they see in terms of my personality. They don't look at the records. I didn't have a bad academic record or anything, but I just have a tendency to think of myself as not very bright.

FROST: What was the first big thing you did?

VOIGHT: Well, I started out in stock. And I was successful on the basis of all those little improvisations and fooling around; but the first big thing was after I had gone through a lot of study, and I finally did *View from the Bridge* off-Broadway, which was another accent role. I played with an

Italian accent. The young blond Italian. And it was after I'd done quite a lot of work in acting and it all kind of came together under a good director, Ulu Grosbard. And that made me a kind of reputation for being a good actor.

FROST: What year was that?

VOIGHT: That was in '64. So it was quite a time. I graduated in 1960, and it was four years later that I got through that big swamp, and finally did something that people said, "Yes, Jon, you have a little talent."

FROST: And when was *Midnight Cowboy* filmed? '67 or '68?

VOIGHT: '68.

FROST: So then there were four more years of struggle. Were they difficult or easy years?

VOIGHT: Well, once I had done that show and I knew that I was good, I had a little more confidence in myself. And I got jobs rather easily, but I was sometimes very bad. I've always had great imagination, and I wanted to try everything that I could. So I did some of the most unbelievably ludicrous performances ever performed on the American stage.

FROST: What sort?

VOIGHT: Well, when I was in stock, after the first year which was fairly successful, they asked me back for a second, and they said, "We'll offer you these roles." I said, "No, no. I feel strong now. I've been in the city, and I've worked very hard on my acting for a year. And I think I'm prepared to do all the leads this season. And if you don't want to talk to me about that, then I don't want to talk to you." And I sat back in my apartment. I waited for the phone call. And it came a little late, but it was there, and he said, "Okay, you can do it." And then I got involved with a girl, and I didn't learn my lines. And I had four leading roles.

FROST: With the girl?

(*Laughter*)

VOIGHT: You know what happened? My most modest role of the season was *Death of a Salesman*, in which I played Happy, which is not the real lead in the play, but it was my

63

warm-up. I figured, "I'll start with that one and then I'll go on to the three leads, *Golden Fleecing*, which has more lines than Hamlet, and a couple of other big ones." When I started out with this first effort, I was working on the Method—and I was doing a lot of things in terms of emotional recall and sensory work, and I really thought I was—God, I just got to be terrific because this is the first time Vermont has ever seen this kind of work, you know.

(*Laughter*)

I really believed this line. And I was concentrating, and on opening night I fainted almost. The reviews came out, and they said, "The show is brilliant. Everyone is urged to go to see it. All the members of the cast are quite extraordinary, with the one exception of Mr. Voight, who can neither walk nor talk."

(*Laughter*)

I was hurt by that review. And then it got worse. I went downhill from there because not only was I unable to walk or talk but I couldn't remember my lines. And it was a tough season. My parents came up to see the show. And I was anxious to see if maybe there wasn't something wrong with the reviewer, some extraordinary bias. And they came up on Sunday to see it, with a girl who was my demise. They saw the show, and we went out afterward and no one talked to me, except my mother came up to me and said, "Jon, no matter what anyone tells you, you were fine."

(*Laughter*)

And I said, "Thank you, Mom." And I got in the car and no one said a word. And my father was in the front seat, and we were down the road about ten miles toward their motel, and we were going to have a drink, and people were talking about everything else. Finally I said, "Dad, I think it's time you said something about my performance. I can take it. Tell me, how bad was it?" And he said, "My advice to you, Jon, is go for a swim. When we get to the motel go for a swim."

FROST: What did the girl say about it?

64

VOIGHT: She loved me.

(*Laughter*)

FROST: How long did you prepare for the part in *Midnight Cowboy?*

VOIGHT: I had read the book about five years earlier, so I just was sitting around thinking about it for a long time. It was probably the only part that I really wanted to do. I turned down an awful lot of things. But finally when we got to it, and they gave me the role, we had a couple weeks' preproduction shooting in New York. I had a week with a voice coach in New York, fellow by the name of J. B. Smith who did a lot of accents. And then I went down to Texas and I spent a week in Texas. And then when I came back, we rehearsed for I think fourteen or eleven days, and then started shooting.

FROST: How much of you is there in the character in *Midnight Cowboy?*

VOIGHT: I really don't know. I think it's easy for me to be Joe Buck. It's almost more comfortable for me to be Joe Buck now than it is for me to be me. I like him a lot. But he goes on his own steam, as a character does when it takes off.

FROST: What kind of experiences did you have in Texas?

VOIGHT: Well, I did very cliché things in a way. I'd say, "I'm going out tonight to a bar, and I'm going to sit there and talk with the people." Now they have liquor bars in Texas, and then they have beer bars, and I went to a beer bar. And I sat there, and there was one guy sitting there, and somebody listening to the jukebox, and me. And I'm waiting for a conversation to start up so I can just maybe get into the accent a little bit. A half an hour goes by, and he doesn't say anything. And we're nodding to the music and tapping out a few things and looking at each other. "I'll have another beer, please." He looks up at me. Like we had some kind of thing going. I don't know what it was.

(*Laughter*)

And then finally I said, "You in cattle?" He said, "Oil."

FROST: He ad-libbed.

VOIGHT: Yeah. "Oil." "Oil, oh." "Yeah." Another half an hour.

(*Laughter*)

It was like that. I mean it was a whole night like that, see. And it was funny. We talked about the water.

(*Laughter*)

VOIGHT: I said, "The water's hard here in this part of Texas." He said, "Yeah, it's good for your second teeth, though."

(*Laughter*)

And then I went to a boot shop and worked there with a bunch of people, and I really got to love them. They knew that I was an actor in town and some of the local characters would stop by this boot shop in Stanton, Texas. They were terrific guys. They'd be these old guys that'd come in. They have nothing to do, see, and they're just sitting by the drugstore up the street. And they'd come in and say something about the weather. They say, "The wind's down."

(*Laughter*)

I can't really represent them properly because they make jokes about the wind, and they'd come in with a little thing they had to say. And it was really sweet. Really nice people. And I talked with this fellow by the name of Otis Williams, who was maybe nearly seventy. He used to be a bronc buster in the rodeo. We talked for long periods of time, and he wanted me to go to a rodeo with him, and I wanted to go, but I knew that we had to leave shortly, and I didn't think I was going to be able to make it. I found out later that he'd gotten tickets for me, and really was excited about the fact that I might go, and I feel kind of disappointed that I didn't. Anyway, I was leaving that day, and I said, "Well, Otis, I'll see you. I'm gonna go. You know, maybe I'll be back in New York. Maybe I'll come up and see the rodeo. I'd like to. But, you know, if I don't, it's been real good talking." So I walked out of the store, and I'm getting in my car. And Otis comes out of the shop with his saddle, and he's walking away. And it's like he wanted to say goodbye, because he probably knew that I wasn't going to see him again, right?

So I walked over toward the car, and Otis walked this way and said, "Yep." And he looked at me, and I said, "Yep." And we stood there for a long time. And he's looking and trying to think of something nice to say. And I didn't know what to say either, but here we were alone in the street of this old ghost town of a place, this old cowboy and me. And I'm standing there, and he finally looks up at me and says, "There's a lot of good horseflesh up there."

(*Laughter*)

It was really touching.

FROST: And good for your second teeth, too. Jon, what's it been like after the fantastic success of *Midnight Cowboy*? You've become a sort of youth-sex, or sex-youth, symbol. Did the reaction knock you out when it first happened?

VOIGHT: I suffered a lot of different reactions. When something like that hits, it hits very heavily for me. I was really unprepared for it. A lot of things happened. Like when I walk down the street, and somebody who knows the work and understands it and likes Joe Buck maybe as much as I like him says, "Hey, terrific!" And he walks on. That's a great feeling.

I came in today to check something, and I walked out front, and a bus driver was driving by, and he said, "Hey, Joe! How you doing?" I said, "Terrific!" That kind of acceptance is a really nice thing to feel. But I'm an actor, and I feel that I have to keep trying other characters. Maybe Joe's the only one I'll ever feel that I ever fulfilled. But I just have to keep going and keep trying other things and getting interested in other things and trying to make those things work. I'll succeed and I'll fail and I'll fool around a little bit.

FROST: You said something about when the movie first hit you almost wanted to hide.

VOIGHT: Yeah, I did. I didn't know what I could follow it with, it was so big. I almost don't want to follow it. It says so many nice things that I really like, and it's so powerful a

67

movie. It's like I want to take a break for a while. But I also want to prove that I'm fallible too. I was thinking of going back on the stage right away and just test my stage legs again. Somebody said, "Why don't you do *Streetcar?* And I wanted to try *Streetcar,* but I'm not right for it in many ways. I could build up to it, like I built up to *Cowboy,* and have a lot of fun doing it. I thought, why not? And then I thought, well, somebody's going to say, "There he is. That's Jon Voight. He's a fifth-rate Marlon Brando." And I'm going to say, "Hey! Wait a minute. Third-rate!"

(*Laughter*)

How Do You Climb to the Top of the Tube
Without Slipping?

◆

Johnny Carson

FROST: Heeeere's Johnny!

(*Music, applause*)

Great to have you with us. Welcome.

CARSON: Thank you, David. You know, this is like coming home, really.

FROST: Yes, this theater is your old home.

CARSON: We did five years of a show in the afternoon called *Who Do You Trust?* It ran from 1956 until I took over the *Tonight Show.*

FROST: How many shows did you do?

CARSON: We probably did almost a thousand shows out of this theater. It was a half-hour comedy interview.

FROST: According to the stories, you had wild guests on those shows. One woman tried to teach you to breathe through your toes.

CARSON: Strange people, yeah. There are a lot of strange people around. And we would put ads in the *Village Voice.* "You want to be on a television show?" Well, this brings out the nuts. (*Laughter*) We had a dentist once who was a complete vegetarian. And he had his office on Central Park South. And during his lunch hour, he would go and have his lunch in the park, which was grass. (*Laughter*) This is a nice man, who, you know, does surgery—No, I don't mean that kind of grass. No, no. (*Laughter*) See how things have changed? Twelve years ago you could say "grass." Somebody would say, "Oh, mow the grass." Now you say "grass,"

69

everybody goes (*coughs*), "Yeah." (*Laughter*) No, he would go over and nibble the grass in Central Park.

FROST: Did he eat anything else?

CARSON: I don't know. I didn't know him intimately, David.

(*Laughter*)

FROST: You're a great reader, aren't you? What are you reading at the moment?

CARSON: I try to be because, you know, when you have, as you do, a great turnover of guests who are in all different areas, you can't read everything as much as you'd like to. You have scientists and politicians and doctors. I think I probably read more nonfiction. I'm reading a book by J. B. Priestley now called *Time and Man*, and I read books on astronomy and one on the population explosion, by a gentleman I've had on the show. Just about anything.

FROST: Your lady wife mentioned that you've been consulting volume fourteen of the *Encyclopaedia Britannica*.

CARSON: I was looking. I was watching a late movie one night with Victor Mature. And I really wanted to see if that happened.

FROST: I used to always have great faith in encyclopedias when I was at school. My father and mother had a set of encyclopedias, and I thought they were just the greatest things on earth.

CARSON: I have the *Britannica*. What do you have, the *Americana*? (*Laughter*)

FROST: Chambers, I think it was, or something like that. Some sort of vaguely scatological name. I was reading it and I thought it was just the greatest book ever until I was writing an essay once on Gladstone. I thought, "I'll write an excellent essay." Until I turned to the end of it, and it said, "Gladstone retired as prime minister and now lives just outside Guildford." You know, I suddenly realized it was about eighty years old.

(*Laughter*)

70

CARSON: You know, getting ready for your show is the strangest. You were kind enough to tender the invitation about a month ago, when I talked with you. But you know something? Your whole staff sounds like you. His producer called. He says (*imitates Frost*), "Super that you could be with us," you know? (*Laughter*) "David's really very thrilled about it, and how would you like to come over?" And I said, "Thank you." And your secretary called. She said (*imitates Frost*), "What a joy that you could all join us on the show." (*Laughter*) Everybody on your staff sounds like you! Weird.

FROST: I'm very touched by that. You're great at impersonations and impressions. Now, what's your very first memory of life? The first thing you can remember.

CARSON: The doctor.

FROST: Slapping you?

CARSON: Yeah.

FROST: Fantastic memory.

CARSON: He had me by the wrong end . . . no, I just made that up. I don't know, it's funny when you go back and try to remember. A lot of people I know say they can go back to three. I just don't remember that far.

FROST: Which of your parents influenced you most? They're still alive?

CARSON: Both my parents are alive. My grandfather's still alive. He was ninety-five this month.

FROST: So you've got four generations.

CARSON: That's right. My folks are not from show business. I'm from the Midwest. I was born in Iowa, lived in Nebraska. My mother, when she was younger, played the piano for a while in a movie theater when she was quite young. You know, it was background music for motion pictures. But none of the folks were in the entertainment business.

FROST: So how do you think you made that choice?

CARSON: I don't know. I was actually always kind of a shy person when I was a kid. Most people don't ever imagine

71

anybody in the entertainment business being withdrawn or shy, but I think I probably was, and you compensate. I think you go the other way. You become the clown. You find, perhaps, you can get laughs when you're a kid, when you're in grade school or high school, and the people laugh at what you do.

FROST: And one of the first places you did things was one of the first places I performed. Methodist socials.

CARSON: Your father's a Methodist preacher. Didn't you study to be a preacher once?

FROST: Yes, I used to give some addresses and read lessons when I was eighteen.

CARSON: The Methodist church. Thrilling, isn't it?

FROST: Yes. You did socials, didn't you?

CARSON: Oh, yes, I played all the church socials, Rotary Clubs. Moose Lodges; you've never lived until you've played the Moose Lodge on Saturday night.

FROST: Oh, really?

CARSON: They can't wait until you get off because the stripper comes out. I played all those things. I started by doing amateur magic when I was about thirteen or fourteen.

FROST: How long did you continue to be John Carson? When did you become Johnny?

CARSON: I think I changed it when I was working in Omaha, in 1948–49. I changed it to John. I guess I liked the feeling of it a little better. John always sounded a little formal. Then it just slowly became Johnny again.

FROST: What memories do you have of the early radio days?

CARSON: Being broke. I went to the radio station when I got out of college, doing a morning radio show, disc jockey show, opened the station at 5:55, did a radio show.

FROST: But you did the commercials and everything?

CARSON: Everything.

FROST: And you started a campaign? Something about pigeons?

CARSON: That's right. They always have these anti-pigeon

campaigns and they were trying to drive them off of the Douglas County Courthouse. You'll get letters now from nice little old ladies who like to, you know, feed the pigeons.

I took the pigeons' side, and did a show from the top of the courthouse, interviewing the pigeons on why they should stay. Interviewed them, you know, with records of coos and so forth. We got them a new building.

FROST: That was the first successful on-air campaign?

CARSON: Yeah, kind of crazy stuff like that.

FROST: And then you went to seek fame and fortune in California. And the first big thing in Hollywood was Red Skelton, was it?

CARSON: I did local shows out there. I started as an announcer and I did a local comedy show on television which I wrote while I was an announcer. Skelton came a few years later.

FROST: And you wrote for him?

CARSON: Yeah. Monologues for Red.

FROST: What kind of a thing did you find yourself writing in those days?

CARSON: Well, it's funny, when you write for somebody else. It's easy to write for yourself because you know what you do. But Red is one of the great clowns working today. Without a doubt, he's a physical comedian. He does great sight gags, and my wife almost went crazy because I found myself sitting at home at night doing, "Do-do-do-do," and she'd say, "What the hell are you doing?" I was used to writing jokes but Red would do these two seagulls. So, I would sit there at home and go, "Do-do-do-do, Gertrude said to Heathcliff, do-do-do-do." And it wasn't painful, it was fun.

But I remember I gave Red a joke once. This was right at the time that Arthur Godfrey had fired Julius LaRosa on the air. Remember that? On his radio show. It was also at the same time that Arthur Godfrey had buzzed the tower at Teterboro Airport. He had taken off against instructions from the tower, and the stories were both in the news.

So I wrote this wonderful joke, because everybody was

73

picking on Arthur Godfrey. Red would come out and say in front of the audience, "Everybody's picking on Arthur Godfrey. It really wasn't his fault about the airport thing. The Julius LaRosa Fan Club had pushed the tower onto the runway," which was a pretty funny and current joke, right?

So, Red walks out, and finishes the joke: "It wasn't Arthur's fault. The Perry Como Fan Club pushed the tower on the runway," and that got one of the biggest laughs I've ever heard in my life, and I've never figured it out. It didn't seem to make any difference, whether it was Perry Como or Dr. Schweitzer who had pushed it on.

FROST: Are there shows of yours you look back on particularly fondly?

CARSON: One of the first shows I ever did in California. It was a local show in Los Angeles called *Carson's Cellar*. I think the reason I enjoyed it was because it was new. It was my first major exposure on the air.

I set myself a time limit, because I don't believe that old show-business cliché that talent will out. You see too many people who keep grinding away year after year.

So, I set myself kind of a time limit. I said, I'll go out to Los Angeles, and I went as an announcer, and I said, if I don't have my own show within a year, I'll chuck it and go back to Omaha.

And I did have. Everything fell into place, and while I was doing the announcing stint, I would sit down and write this show. Strangely enough, it was very comparable with what I'm doing right now, a potpourri of everything, people, comedy, sketches, stand-up monologue. I was kind of fond of that show because we did it on a very low budget and worked with a lot of great people.

I was able some way to inveigle Fred Allen into appearing on the show, and he came on with a piece of material of his own and performed it. A great thing for me at that time.

FROST: How long did you do that program?

CARSON: I think that show was on for twenty-six weeks, only locally in Los Angeles, and then from that it kicked off a couple of network things.

74

FROST: And when you came to take over the *Tonight Show*, I gather everybody said, "Don't do it."

CARSON: I turned the *Tonight Show* down the first time it was offered to me because the show here was very comfortable, quite easy. I'd come in at two, we would do the show, I'd be through at four. It was not a bad existence, and they were paying me fairly good money for that kind of a show.

When the *Tonight Show* came up, Jack Paar had had such a great success with it and was such a unique personality, my first reaction was, "Why do you need that kind of trouble? It's nice here and it's comfortable."

But then I thought it over and I said, "Well, gee, if you're really going to take a shot at it, you ought to be willing to either grab all the marbles or get out of the business."

So I accepted. I had reservations about it because following Jack was tough. He'd put such a unique stamp on it. And it takes a while to overcome that and make it your own show.

FROST: Did you deliberately make it different right from the start?

CARSON: You only make it different because you change the people. The format of the *Tonight Show*, any talk show, is basically the same. You have a location, you have people. It doesn't make any difference whether you do it standing up, lying down, or on the floor.

FROST: You mentioned that you were getting quite good money when you were doing *Who Do You Trust?* I get the impression that while money is an important measure of your success, money itself isn't very important to you, is it?

CARSON: Not in that sense. I think the only thing that money gives you is the fact that it gives you the freedom of not having to worry about money.

FROST: Let's talk a bit about you. Do you think you are religious?

CARSON: I don't know whether I am or not, but I don't think that what you believe in is important. Behavior has more to do with it. Everybody can believe in something, but it all comes down to behavior, in the long run.

FROST: You mean you really believe more in the ability of human beings than in any God?

CARSON: Yes. Saying "I'm a Catholic, I'm a Jew, I'm a Protestant, and I believe in a Creator or a Supernatural Being" isn't important. If it works for you, fine. But I think it's easy to believe in anything, but how you handle yourself as a human being is what counts. I sound like Billy Graham all of a sudden.

FROST: Do you think there is any supernatural force out there at all?

CARSON: I haven't the foggiest. I think Pascal said a man would be a fool not to believe in God. He said if you believe in God, fine. You've got it made. But not to believe, he says, you might as well take it and believe anyway. He may be right. I don't know. If there is no God, you have nothing to worry about, and if there is, you're covered.

W. C. Fields didn't profess to be a religious man, but when he was in his final days and in a home in Encino, California, dying of the alcohol, Gene Fowler, his good friend, saw him reading the Bible. Fowler asked, "Bill, what are you doing?" And Fields said, "Looking for loopholes."

I love that. Maybe Pascal was right. If there isn't a God, it doesn't make any difference, and if there is, you're in like a porch climber.

FROST: Do you think life's easier for young people today or more difficult?

CARSON: I think it's tougher today. School is tougher. Education is tougher. Colleges are certainly a lot more competitive today, and I think life, generally, for youngsters is a little more uptight than it was.

FROST: Talking about relationships, you said once to one of your children—

CARSON: I get the feeling that you're St. Peter and I'm trying to get into heaven. You've got my whole dossier here, and if I blow one of these questions, I ain't gonna get in.

(*Laughter*)

76

FROST: You've got four stars. You were talking with your son about whether a boy should sleep with a girl or not. You said that the question to ask was, "Is the boy ready to accept the responsibility of that relationship, and is the girl?"

CARSON: I think youngsters today are much more honest about what they're doing. I simply do not believe that there is a decrease in sexual morality. People are simply talking about sex more. The same things happened in college and high school some time ago. People just weren't as open about it. Some people say, "The birth-control pill has brought on all this permissiveness." I don't think it has at all, from people I have talked with. The only difference is they don't get pregnant now.

FROST: Do you think there's less guilt about all these things now?

CARSON: I hope there is. I think there ought to be. Guilt and anxiety about sexual relationships, and people saying what they should not do, cause the biggest hangups in the world. It's like holding a cake up in front of a fifteen- or sixteen-year-old boy and saying, "There's the cake, but you can't eat that until you're twenty-one. Well, that's wonderful but it just doesn't work, you know.

(*Laughter*)

Because they're ready at sixteen and seventeen and eighteen and nineteen and twenty and what you're trying to tell them in effect is the law does not permit you to partake of this thing that you sell on television and in the newspapers and in the motion pictures. You can't touch that. That's a no-no. When the glands are saying that's a yes-yes!

(*Laughter and applause*)

FROST: A tribute to J.C. This is a fantastic quote of yours. "My kids once asked me what words I considered to be bad"—in relationship to four-letter words, I guess—"I told them the bad words were 'nigger,' 'kike,' 'greaseball' and 'wop.'"

CARSON: One day I think we were discussing bad language, euphemisms for sexual intercourse, parts of the body, et cetera. I asked my boys, "Well, just for the fun of it, why don't you tell me every dirty word that you know." We sat around, and one of them would say, dot-dot-dot. One of them, dot-dot-dot. You know, like they were saying something that nobody'd ever heard, and they kind of giggled, and I said, "No, those really aren't dirty words. They don't have really any generic meaning. You can use the word for copulation and it can be an adjective, a noun, an adverb, depending on how you want to use it. It's only a word." And I said, "Your real dirty words are 'wop,' 'nigger,' 'kike,' 'dago,' et cetera, because those words have emotional meaning, and they hurt." I said, "That's the point. The other words really don't mean anything. If you want to say them, you can say them all you want to. It just shows that you don't have a very good command of the English language. It's only the connotation that you put on them, as far as I'm concerned. But those words that hurt, that have an emotional attachment to them, those are the words that are unpleasant to me.

FROST: I absolutely agree.

(*Applause*)

FROST: If you were to give up the *Tonight Show* for something or other, what would you like to crusade for?

CARSON: It'd probably be for population control.

FROST: Because you feel that's what's threatening us all?

CARSON: Well, it really is.

FROST: Yes. Do you think anything can be done about that?

CARSON: Yes, you stop (*bleep*).

(*Laughter and applause*)

FROST: That's it.

CARSON: I've always wanted to say that, and I didn't have the chance. That's really not fair to you, David. That was not a professional thing to do. Could I soften it a little bit? It was not a very classy way to put it. You know, everybody uses that word, all the time. I'm sure they use that word more than probably any other four-letter word in the world. But it was probably out of context here.

FROST: Sort of right in context.

CARSON: Yes, it certainly was.

FROST: The problem is that since the glands are saying yes-yes that plan might not work.

CARSON: No, it probably won't work. I had a very brilliant young biologist on the show by the name of Paul Erlich. He brought up this point that if you don't limit the population somewhere along the line, inevitably it will become an unbearable situation of just too many people.

FROST: But everybody says that your show, by keeping everybody up, is contributing to that.

CARSON: We have a lot of commercials, David.

SOCIAL QUESTIONS, PERTINENT AND IMPERTINENT

◆

SOME AMERICANS have a pretty drastic remedy for the social ills of our time. The American revolutionary, Abbie Hoffman, announced he is a "heavenist" and that the key to his heaven on earth is first "a struggle with a dying death culture" followed by the abolition of "that dirty four-letter word called work. I mean, we demand full unemployment."

When I asked him if he had a hero, he replied, "Well, I like the Marx Brothers, all of them, including Karl. I think the revolution we are talking about is as American as a MacDonald's hamburger. The only difference is it has more meat."

The American Conservative—William Buckley—was naturally somewhat less apocalyptic. "It depends completely what you focus on. Life can't be all bad when for ten dollars you can buy all the Beethoven sonatas and listen to them for ten years."

Nevertheless, returning to America, he found the loneliness "as three-dimensional as this chair" and was led to the conclusion that "one of these days people are going to discover, you know, Christianity."

Religious faith still is an issue in America of the 70s—not just by its presence and the form it takes (one of Archbishop Fulton Sheen's concerns), but even more perhaps by its absence. By what has replaced it. For some it is a faith in country, or in psychiatry, or in astrology, or in straightforward human improvability. But wherever there is a void, something fills it.

Jane Fonda spoke for many, perhaps, when she said, "If you asked me what's the one thing in the whole world I would like more than anything else, it's for even fifty seconds to be able to—pow—be in someone's head and just see the world through their eyes."

We take a look at the social mosaic of America through the eyes of a judge, a consumers' crusader, a former attorney-general, a Roman Catholic archbishop, and a proud Southerner who is also editor of *Harper's* magazine.

Should the Death Penalty Be Brought Back Quickly?

◆

Judge Samuel Leibowitz

LEIBOWITZ: You look like a fellow that I sentenced about two months ago.

(*Laughter*)

FROST: How much did I get?

LEIBOWITZ: Thirty to sixty.

FROST: Days or years?

LEIBOWITZ: Years. Oh, no, no. I'm not serious. You look like an honest man.

FROST: That's good to know. Thank God for that. Judge Leibowitz, which was the case you're proudest of in all your career as a lawyer?

LEIBOWITZ: The Scotsboro case. It started back in 1931. There were two white girls, tramps, prostitutes, who had shacked up with some white hobos in Chattanooga, Tennessee, in the Hobo's Jungle. The following day they decided to go back to their hometown in Huntsville, Alabama, and they boarded an open railroad car called a gondola, I think. There were some black boys and some white boys in the car, and they got into a scrap. And the black boys put the white boys off the gondola. And the white boys went back to the railroad station they had just passed and complained to the sheriff, and the sheriff telephoned down the line to stop the train.

The train stopped at Paint Rock, Alabama. And there was a posse there, some forty or fifty gentlemen armed to the teeth. Three of the Negro boys escaped, and nine were captured. And these two female tramps—they were convicted prostitutes—set up a cry that they had been raped. Six raped one and six raped the other. These Negroes had put a knife up to their throats. They had punched them and knocked them down and kicked them and each one was raped by six Negroes.

The girls were taken to a doctor's office to be examined. In fact, two doctors examined them, found there was absolutely nothing the matter with them. There wasn't even a sign of any violence. They claimed they were beaten and cuffed and manhandled, and there wasn't a sign of it.

But nonetheless these boys were taken to Scotsboro, which was the county seat. The youngest was thirteen, and the oldest was seventeen. And the Klan came down there, and they raised the devil. They had a band. They played *The Gang's All Here*. And they shouted and they ranted, while the trial was going on. In four days, eight of these boys were convicted and sentenced to Alabama's electric chair, in spite of the fact that the doctors testified that there was no evidence of any rape.

The ninth boy was given life imprisonment because he was only thirteen years of age at the time. Well, the case went up to the United States Supreme Court, which unanimously reversed the convictions on the grounds that there was this mob outside of the courthouse inflaming the jury. They set aside the conviction also because the boys were not properly represented by counsel. And then I entered the case in 1933. Well, it'll take hours to go through the details in the case. I'll just touch one or two of the highlights.

These girls testified before Mr. Justice James Horton. If ever a man looked and acted like Abraham Lincoln it was Judge Horton. The case was tried, and these defendants were convicted, and during the trial I raised the point about them keeping Negroes off juries, which was in violation of the Constitution. And I put on witnesses to show that there were qualified Negroes to serve on the jury, but Judge Horton denied the motion. Then the defendants were convicted, and out of a blue sky Judge Horton set the conviction aside. On the specific ground that these two prostitutes had lied their heads off. And that these boys were innocent of this crime. But instead of dismissing the indictments, which he should have done, he directed that they have a new trial.

This time it was before Mr. Justice William Washington Callahan. Oh, he gave me a hard time, but I kept my cool. I didn't rant. I took my exceptions, and finally I raised this question again about keeping Negroes off the jury. And what do you think happened? They brought in a volume, a tome, a jury roll with the names of the jurors. At the bottom of seven pages were the names of seven Negro people. Just a forgery. And the object was to prevent me from going to the United States Supreme Court.

Well, to make a long story short, we finally wound up in Washington, and the conviction was reversed on the ground that the State of Alabama had denied the black man his rights to serve on the jury, and that these names were forged on the jury rolls. So after a period of time, all of these defendants were let go except one who escaped from a prison farm. He was later killed in Cleveland, I believe. That's the story of the Scotsboro case. It was a milestone in the history of America. After the Dred Scott decision this was the case which started the Negro on the road to getting his civil rights.

A funny thing happened. After I became a judge, Mrs. Leibowitz and I used to go down to Florida to spend Christmas vacation. On a rainy day, I took a walk along the boulevard there and stopped at the Dade County Court House. There was not much doing there. Just one trial. And as I sat there in the empty chairs, nobody was there but the partisans, the people that were engaged in the trial, and I looked into the jury box, and I saw a Negro. During one of the recesses I motioned for the lawyer to come over to where I was sitting. I said, "I'm from the North. I'm a stranger here. I see you have a colored man on the jury." He said, "Yes, if it weren't for that (*bleep*) Leibowitz, we wouldn't have any niggers on the jury."

(*Laughter and applause*)

FROST: That's a great story. Tell me, you once defended Al Capone, didn't you?

LEIBOWITZ: I defended him for murder in Brooklyn. He allegedly killed three people in a speakeasy in South Brooklyn, and then when he got into trouble in Chicago with the income tax people, he sent for me to confer with the counsel that represented him in Chicago. I went out to Chicago.

There's something about these big gangsters. Capone, Bruno Richard Hauptmann, with whom I spent sixteen hours in the death house in Trenton, Charlie Luciano, Albert Anastasia, whom I defended for murder on three occasions, Vincent Coll, the Mad Dog of the underworld. I'll name the whole litany of the top characters.

FROST: Such as . . .

LEIBOWITZ: Buggsy Siegel, Pittsburgh Coal Strauss. You name them.

FROST: You name them.

(*Laughter*)

LEIBOWITZ: You know, David, there's something that's almost unbelievable about these people. There's a strain of femininity in them. They're lachrymose. Capone said, "Would you like to go to the racetrack?" when I was out in Chicago. I said, "Certainly." So I got into his Cadillac and we drove through the Loop. His window was down. He was driving. They could have killed him in a second. In the back seat sat a gentleman known as Frankie Lake, otherwise known as Machine Gun Jack McGern.

(*Laughter*)

And we rode through Cicero. Cicero is a little town outside of Chicago on the way to the racetrack. He said, "You know, Mr. Leibowitz, I feel good today." I said, "Why, Al?" He said, "I got up early this morning, and I went out to the cemetery. We built a beautiful mausoleum for my brother Ralph, who was killed here in Cicero in an election riot." He says, "I had a good cry." He says, "Now I feel good." That's Al Capone.

If you met Al Capone, it wasn't the Al Capone that the novels write about or the television or moving pictures show. He was just like a big overgrown boy. He didn't use any four-letter words. And if he was sitting here in this audience, he'd be lost in the shuffle.

Now, there's one story about Al. Two of his henchmen had snitched on him. Turned rat, as they call it. And they had gone to jail for some crime, and when they finished their terms there was a big line-up of cars to await their returning brethren, and they were escorted over to a restaurant. They were dined and wined and finally Capone said, "Let's go into the music room." They went into the music room and they sang, and finally Al said, "Let these two boys get down on their knees and sing 'Hallelujah.'" And the two of them went down on their knees, and somebody handed Capone a base-ball bat and he bat the brains out of both of them. Right then and there to show the rest of the mob what happens to a squealer.

You take Bruno Hauptmann, the man that killed the Lind-bergh baby. He had a picture of his own little boy on a shelf in the death house. And when he'd talk about him, the tears would roll down his cheeks. And then when I talked to him about the crime itself, the eyes would recede, and it was the most ghoulish appearance. That's characteristic of almost all of these big-time criminals. They have a lachrymose instinct in them.

FROST: If they're naturally lachrymose, what made them into big shots?

LEIBOWITZ: Oh, gosh, David, if I could answer that ques-tion. The psychiatrists and the psychologists have been pon-dering over that matter for many many years. You see, it starts when they're young. Juvenile delinquents. May I say something about juvenile delinquents?

FROST: Yes, you may.

LEIBOWITZ: I was born in Rumania. I came here when I was four years old. My father was a pushcart peddler. We lived on Essex Street in the heart of the East Side. If you think

Harlem has slums, you should have seen the slums that my parents and I lived in. The sixth floor of a tenement, no bathrooms, no baths. The toilet was in the hallway for the six tenants on the floor. And in the wintertime, when the toilet was out of order you had to go down the six flights of steps through the snow to the outhouse. There were no psychiatrists in those days, no psychologists, no social workers, no welfare. And still people got along because we lived in the community. And everybody in the community knew everybody else.

A girl wouldn't dare to go wrong because the neighbors would be talking about it, and fingers would be pointed at her, and the family would have to move out.

We obeyed the cop's mandate, take a walk. The father was respected. Nobody lifted a spoon at the table until Pop sat in his chair. That was his chair. He could have been the worst bum in the world, but he was respected. The mother respected the father. The mother didn't wear the pants the way some women do today.

(*Laughter*)

No, there was a father image, and the child was taught to respect authority. The authority of the parents, the authority of the policeman, the authority of the teacher. Whoever heard of a teacher being beaten in the classroom? Or inkwells being thrown at her, or four-letter words being bandied about or riots being created? And they had respect for the courts, for the judges on the bench. They didn't cause any riots in the courtroom, such as happened over in Chicago. No hell was raised in the courts of law. There was respect. There was order. And so kids used to have little troubles. They'd have fights with the kids next block, or they'd break a window, or they'd steal lumber for the election bonfires, which some of us older people remember. But whoever heard of children being tried for murder? I've tried them for murder at the age of fifteen. And sixteen!

I remember when I was a kid lawyer: on arraignment day, when you bring in the new cases, there were men thirty-five, forty, forty-five. Twenty-five was young. Today if they wore kneepants as they did in the olden days, you'd find a veritable procession of kneepanted kids being brought up before the bar of justice for the most hideous, vicious crimes that you can think of. That's what happened to our blessed country. And my heart is broken. And these people in this audience who have lived in those days, who know what we had in those days compared to what is going on today, are sick at heart. Our hearts are bleeding for this blessed country of ours that we love.

This country gave me everything that I've had. I was, as I said, a little immigrant kid from Rumania. After Hitler got into power, I would have been dead if I hadn't come to this country. And here I became a Justice of the Supreme Court because of the opportunities that this glorious country of ours gives every man.

(*Applause*)

Frost: Tell me, courtrooms are incredibly dramatic places, but what do you look back on as the funniest moment?

Leibowitz: I'll tell you a funny story. There was a family fighting in Borough Park. And the brother-in-law was there and the husband was there and the wife was there, and the brother-in-law ran out and brought back a cop. In uniform. And the claim was that the husband was behind the curtains, and when the cop came into the place to settle the argument, he came from behind the curtains with a gun, and he shot at the policeman, and then ran away.

About a year and a half after this happened, this individual came to my office. His name was Marino, I think. He said, "I understand the police are looking for me. They claim that I shot at a policeman. I never had anything to do with the police. I haven't been living at home for a year and a half." I said, "Where were you all this time?" He said, "I was working in a fish market." I said, "Remember, when you come to court, you better know all about fish."

(*Laughter*)

Well, the case came to trial, and he took the witness chair.

And he said he was working in the fish market all of this time. The moment the words "fish market" came out of his mouth, the prosecutor leaned over to his assistant, and I said to myself, ah, they're going out for a basket of fish. Sure enough, in came the gentleman with a basket of fish, and they laid out some twelve on the table. And the district attorney lifted up the first fish and he says, "Tell me, what is this fish?" And he stared and stared and stared and the district attorney snapped his fingers, and he says, "Come on, you worked in a fish market. What is this fish?" And he says that it's a porgy. But it turned out to be a fiddler. And so he went from fish to fish and the score was zero.

(*Laughter*)

And it looked like curtains for this defendant. Then I got up to sum up. I said, "Gentlemen of the jury, there are four people on this jury that know what a fraud has been perpetrated on my client and on you gentlemen of the jury. Here's a man that worked in Borough Park in a fish market, in a strictly Jewish fish market. Here are twelve fish that are Christian fish. There isn't a single fish that's used by a Jewish housewife to make her gefilte fish. You're trying the man on Christian fish when all he knows is Jewish fish!"

(*Laughter and applause*)

Well, the jury was out about fifteen minutes and they found him not guilty.

(*Laughter*)

Oh, there're so many funny things that happen.

FROST: Can you think of any others?

LEIBOWITZ: Oh, golly, no.

(*Laughter*)

FROST: I never heard anyone say no sounding more like saying yes. You were talking earlier on about sentencing. How many people have you had to sentence to the death penalty? Altogether.

LEIBOWITZ: About forty.

FROST: You're obviously a very warm and human man. Was that a terribly difficult thing to do?

LEIBOWITZ: For some. Not for others.

FROST: You mean sometimes you thought this is not half enough penalty?

LEIBOWITZ: Well, you're a human being, and you have commingling feelings on the subject. I'm a believer in capital punishment.

(*Applause*)

You know, those that wish to abolish capital punishment are organized. And I venture if you stopped a hundred people on the street here, on 44th Street, and took a poll, you'd find that ninety percent are in favor of capital punishment. But they've abolished it in New York State. I think it was wrong, and it's my sober judgment that it is coming back.

(*Applause*)

FROST: Here, we don't want to get into a whole long debate on capital punishment because we want to hear more of your career, but come back to your forty times. How often was it really difficult to do it?

LEIBOWITZ: There were two cases where both the district attorney and I went to Governor Dewey and begged him to commute the sentence. The defendants weren't strictly insane, but they were on the verge of insanity, and the Governor turned us down. Both the district attorney and I went there and the Governor insisted upon their execution. They were.

FROST: Do you think any of the forty were innocent?

LEIBOWITZ: That's a big point that the abolitionists raise all the time. What about executing a man who's innocent? You can't bring him back to life again. Let me say this, that in the entire history of this country, with the thousands that have been executed, there hasn't been a single case ever brought to notice where an innocent man was executed. Not one. It took eleven years to execute Chessman. It'll take years before Mr. Sirhan goes to the chair, if he ever does. We're so careful. There're so many appeals and appeals and appeals.

FROST: But in England there have been one or two cases where people have been wrongly executed.

LEIBOWITZ: I don't know about innocent men in England

having been executed. We haven't had one in America. But capital punishment deters some, s-o-m-e. Not those that killed, those that are in the death houses, but there are some that are deterred, and Mr. Frost, if you want me to prove it, I have the proof right here.

FROST: Well, I'd be delighted to debate it with you because I think if capital punishment does deter that's a very powerful argument in its favor. We had a tremendous debate on the subject in England recently. But nobody could point to any place in the world where it could be proved that capital punishment deters. And one of the main bits of evidence was from Middle America, where there are three states close together: one that's just abolished the death penalty, one that hasn't, and one that has. And the rate of murder in all three is identical. It makes no difference, according to these statistics.

LEIBOWITZ: Statistics don't mean a blessed thing. You want me to prove that capital punishment deters? I've got the official court records right here. It'll only take a minute to read what the defendant said, that he didn't kill because he didn't want to go to the hot seat. He was facing forty years for stickup. He was a third or fourth offender. I said, "Why didn't you shoot the man?" And I've got it right here, in black and white. The court record. And he said, "I didn't want to sit in the hot seat. That's why I didn't kill him."

Not only one case, but I had several cases here. Now, my thesis is this, David: We don't know how many have been deterred, but some have. If I can save the life of one innocent human being whose life is going to be snuffed out by a gunman who wants to take his life, and if the electric chair deters him from taking that human being's life, I'd kill a thousand of them.

(*Applause*)

FROST: Kill a thousand who?

LEIBOWITZ: I'd kill a thousand of those that are cold-blooded killers for gain. I'm not talking about the man that gets into an argument with somebody and kills in the heat of passion. That's not murder in the first degree. That's man-slaughter. But if a man goes out intending to take somebody's life in a cold-blooded fashion for gain, I'd give him the electric chair. But before I did that I would do this. I'd leave it up to the jury. Not make it mandatory. Let the jury decide whether he deserves the chair. Let them go into all facets of his life, to see what kind of a person he is, to see if there are any ameliorating circumstances which would call for life imprisonment instead of the chair. But the electric chair is coming back to this state. It was abolished in eight or nine states. Abolished and restored. Restored because the people wanted it restored. And I think the people of New York State want it restored too.

You talked about England. Let me read you what's happening over in your country.

FROST: Well, I was there last weekend, but—

LEIBOWITZ: Would you mind reading it out to the audience, please. I'll catch my breath when you read it. The last paragraph here. That's from the New York law journal called the *London Letter*.

FROST: "They say that the oddest thing is the reluctance of professional politicians to put their . . ."

LEIBOWITZ: A little louder, Mr. Frost.

(*Laughter*)

FROST: This is my courtroom, not yours.

(*Laughter*)

"The electorate was never consulted," it says, "about the abolition of capital punishment."

LEIBOWITZ: That means the people.

FROST: "Any more than they were consulted about the relaxation of the divorce law, legalization of homosexuality and abortion or the possibility of curbing immigration. The result is an attitude towards politicians which is a combination of resentment and helpless resignation."

Listen, I often share the attitude of resentment and help-less resignation about politics, but it's not simply because of capital punishment. In England the reason that it has been

93

abolished is that when they looked at all the states of Europe and Australia where capital punishment had been abolished, they found it had no effect on the rate of murder. In England, it was therefore concluded that the disadvantages, namely the possibility of innocent men going to the gallows, outweighed it.

LEIBOWITZ: How about London? Do you know the figures of London? I do.

FROST: Yes, I do know the figures of London.

LEIBOWITZ: I give you the figures right from the British Information Service only the other day. Murder has doubled in London since the abolition of capital punishment.

FROST: Wrong.

(*Laughter and applause*)

Murders have increased in London, but if you take away those murders in which people then immediately committed suicide after committing the murder—now you can't argue that someone who commits the murder, then commits suicide, would have been dissuaded by the fact that he was going to be executed, because he's just killed himself—if you take those and the killing of relatives, then the rate is still the same.

I rest my case, your honor.

(*Applause*)

Have you ever broken the law yourself, Sam?

(*Laughter*)

LEIBOWITZ: I take the Fifth Amendment.

(*Laughter*)

I guess there isn't a person in the world that hasn't broken the law. I suppose traffic laws, something of that kind. But what law are you talking about?

FROST: I just wondered. Speeding, perhaps?

LEIBOWITZ: Speeding or parking. Gosh, how much do you have to pay to park your car here in this neighborhood? About three bucks for a couple of hours? Pretty expensive, isn't it?

(*Laughter*)

94

FROST: Did you ever move a court to tears?

LEIBOWITZ: I don't know. You know, cases aren't won with this theatrical business. I want to tell you a little story.

FROST: Good.

LEIBOWITZ: Mrs. Leibowitz and I—the young lady—

FROST: The young lady in the front. Mrs. Leibowitz. Welcome.

(*Applause*)

LEIBOWITZ: Belle and I went to Hollywood a few years ago. The man at the Fox Studio said, "Would you like to see a picture being made?" I said, "Certainly." So he said, "Take the Judge and Mrs. Leibowitz to lot number six." That was the only lot that was working. So we followed this boy down an alleyway and we came to a place that looked like a garage. And there was an electric sign outside which said Silence, Silence, Silence. And he put his finger up to his lips, and we followed him into the building and through a door in the set, and where do you think I found myself? In a courtroom. And gosh, it was the best duplicate of a courtroom I've ever seen in my life. It looked like the old courtroom in General Sessions on Centre Street in New York. The place was dirty. There were cigar butts between the benches on the floor. There were pieces of newspaper out in the corner. The windows were full of dust and full of dirt. You could hardly see the outside through those windows. And there was this spittoon in front of this great desk where he could hit the bull's-eye with the chewing tobacco.

And Joan Crawford was in the chair. She was the witness. She was the defendant. And the lawyer was cross-examining her with the finger. You know, always with the finger. And pirouetting around like a ballet dancer. And every time Joan would answer a question he'd turn to the jury and say, "Gentlemen, she's lying!"

Well, if that ever happened in the court, in any court in the land or in the world, they'd take the jackass lawyer by the seat of his pants and they'd throw him out into the corridor.

95

But they went over and over and over and over the same darn thing. Until I knew the lines by heart. Finally the director said, "Cut." There's a kid came in with two boards, you know, and they cut the boards, and then the thing was over, and the director came over to me. You know who the director was? Otto Preminger. So Mr. Preminger says, "Tell me, Judge, is the flag in the right place?"

(*Laughter*)

I swear. I said, "Mr. Preminger, the flag is in the right place, the spittoon is where it should be, the place is filthy and dirty, the jury box looks exactly like what we have downtown in Centre Street." I said, "Where in hell did you get this shyster lawyer?"

(*Laughter and applause*)

FROST: Tell me, what do you plan to do now you're retired?

LEIBOWITZ: I was thinking of opening up a peanut stand.
(*Laughter*)

In front of the courthouse. Three peanuts in a bag, and I'll autograph each peanut. Fifteen cents a bag. I'm kidding, of course. I'm associated with one of the great trial lawyers in this country, one of the best, Jack Fuchsberg, down at 250 Broadway. And I've got a nice office there. And I putter along. I'm going to do some lecturing.

FROST: Have you got any other particular moments in the courtroom that you particularly relish as you look back over your life as a judge?

LEIBOWITZ: Well, can I tell you about something that's tragic?

FROST: Yes.

LEIBOWITZ: It's what's happened in Chicago. I've been on the bench now twenty-nine years. A long time. And I've lived a million lives. As a lawyer and a judge. And to me what's happened over there is tragic. I'm not going to defend Judge Hoffman, because I wasn't there. I don't know what the testimony was and what his rulings were. He may have been greatly in error. And there's a higher court that

96

will correct whatever mistakes he made. I've been reversed too. There isn't a judge who's on a trial bench during a period of time that hasn't been reversed by a higher court. But the mere fact that a judge has been reversed is meaningless. Now I'm not holding any brief for Judge Hoffman. But it's just sickening to have these people come in there and to call this man a pig and a Hitler and the vilest names that one can use in the gutter.

Now, I've had cases. I've had judges that were tough. I took my exception on the record in a gentlemanly way. The higher courts gave me relief. But to move from the campus riots into the courtroom and create riots there, unless it's stopped, means the end of our system of justice!

(*Applause*)

It wouldn't happen in a million years, David Frost, in your blessed country in Old Bailey! Go into Old Bailey and you see what respect is given to the judge and what respect the lawyers have, and what respect the audience has. And even the man in the dock!

Now the situation in Chicago can't be tolerated. I have the solution. I had a fellow come into my court charged with murder. A gangland murder. This was in the middle of the winter. And he sat down, then he took off his jacket. If he was more comfortable without his jacket, it was all right with me. Then he took off his tie. That was a little peculiar, but maybe he liked it without the tie. Then he stood up and took off his shirt.

(*Laughter*)

And then when he stood up finally he said, "Look at that white-haired ——— sitting up there on the bench." Now I'm giving it to you from the record. So I sent the jury out, and I said to the attorney, I said, "Tell this man to behave himself or I'm going to take action." So they whispered to him and then the jury came back. The minute the jury came back, he started to yodel.

(*Laughter*)

Like a Swiss mountaineer. And there was the devil to pay

97

in the courtroom. Well, I sent for a psychiatrist down in the Kings County Hospital. A lady by the name of Dr. McDermott, and she came there with two gentlemen in white coats, and they had a little package under their arm. I said, "Doctor, look him over. Tell me, is he faking or is he on the up and up?" So she observed him and observed and finally she took the witness stand while the jury was out. She said, "Judge Leibowitz, this fellow is a faker." I said, "Really? Go ahead, do your job." So they wrestled around with him. They put him in a strait jacket. They put a gag in his mouth. They put towels this way and that way. And when they got finished he looked like an Egyptian mummy.

(*Laughter*)

And they sat him down, and I had the arms chained to the chair and the legs to the table, and the trial proceeded. And I said, "You have a right to talk to your lawyer. All you have to do is to tap your foot three times and I'll have the restraints removed." So the minute the trial went ahead he (*Leibowitz taps his foot three times*). I said remove the restraints. So they took all of this stuff off him, and he started to yell at the top of his voice.

The next morning he came in there he wouldn't wear any clothes. And they had to get a horse blanket and wrap the horse blanket around him, with diaper pins to hold it, and all he needed was a feather in his head and he'd look like an Indian.

(*Laughter*)

Well, to make the long story short, it came time for the defense. I said, "Does your client wish to testify?" (*Three raps*) And he took the witness chair, and his feet—no shoes— his feet were dirty, and they smelled.

(*Laughter*)

And he lifted up his foot and shot it over the rail of the witness box, and he hit the stenographer in the head and the stenographer went back on his backside and the ink flew all over the place, and then he wheeled around and he shot his leg toward me. And I almost went back on my rear end. I

98

said, "Take him out of here." Well, eventually he was convicted. He went up to Sing Sing. He called the warden, and he said, "Warden, I couldn't fool that old guy." He says, "I put on an act, but I couldn't fool him." Well, he went to the chair like a little lamb, and when they strapped him into the chair, one of the guards told me, "You know what he said? He said, 'Give my regards to Judge Leibowitz.'" So that ended that.

The South Is a Split Infinitive Trying to Get Together

◆

Willie Morris

FROST: And now it's my great pleasure to welcome the author of the book called *North Toward Home*, the editor of *Harper's* magazine, Mr. Willie Morris!

(*Applause*)

When were you in Mississippi last?

MORRIS: Well, I spent a long time in Mississippi in January, and then again in March, because the State of Mississippi, ironic as it may seem, now has the most thoroughly integrated public school system in America, and they were integrating my old high school in Yazoo City, Mississippi, which is now sixty percent black. And I wanted to be there for that, and so I spent a lot of time there.

I found that really the most touching part of the whole business was the kids themselves, the students.

I have this old ninety-five-year-old grandmother whose great-great uncle was the first governor of Mississippi. I asked her, "Mamie, do you think this is ever going to work, these blacks and whites going to school together?" And she said, "Oh, son, I don't know, I'm not sure. I think it will, if the adults will just leave them alone."

And this is what I found out in Mississippi. They're starting to play basketball and football together, which I think is crucial. You know, there are a lot of Southerners of both races who still believe passionately that racial integration is an expression of the deepest in our ethic as a people.

100

FROST: You went to Yazoo, and you talked about the old warring impulses of one's sensibility, to be both Southern and American. How difficult is that?

MORRIS: Very difficult, especially if you're a writer. I was at a seminar at Yale recently. We were talking to some of the students who were studying literature. And I was with William Styron, and Robert Penn Warren, who's a great man, the only man in American literature who's won Pulitzer prizes in three categories: for fiction, for his great novel *All the King's Men*, for poetry, and also for literary criticism and history.

The three of us were talking to the students, and all the questions were very much to the point, except the last one, when the student addressed his question to me, and said, "I've been listening quite closely to you gentlemen tonight, and I only have one question to ask: why is it that three such seemingly civilized and intelligent men come from such a backward and barbaric region as the American South?"

I said, "On a query of such import, I've got to defer to my distinguished senior, Robert Penn Warren." Robert Penn Warren had the dregs of a bourbon in his hand—this was one of his informal Yale sessions—and he looked down at his ice, and he said, "I'm tired of hearing this question from Yankee intellectuals." And he said, "I guess it just has something to do with innoculation against hookworm."

I do think, David, that there are very deep warring impulses, to be a Southerner. Why is it, for instance, that the South in many ways is the most patriotic part of America, when it comes to fighting the wars: why is it that the South right now—I took my ten-year-old son down to Honor America Day at the Washington Monument, and he applauded Bob Hope, and all the people, and Red Skelton, when he gave the pledge of allegiance to the flag. And I whispered, I said, "David, these people disagree with us politically." And David said, "I don't care, because they put on a good show." Why is it that the South now, for instance, by and large is a great supporter of what I think to be a tragic involvement in Viet-

101

nam. I think it has something to do with a warrior tradition. And with the fact that the American South was the only part of America that has ever suffered defeat.

I think it's no accident that the generals, the soldiers, the professionals, so many of them are from rural areas of the South. I might disagree with them politically, but I find, you know, a real irony there.

FROST: What do you think is the future for racism? Will it prosper or fall by the way?

MORRIS: I think racism is so deeply ingrained in the American people. I feel quite strongly that people from the American South, both whites and blacks, understand all the nuances and the complexities, and the terrible workings out of racism in a way that we find it hard to explain to our fellow Americans, or to Europeans.

I think it'll always be with us. You know, in some ways I believe that for a person, or indeed for a society, to become truly civilized, involves overcoming one's deepest instincts and shortcomings.

On the other hand, we have to achieve some working, day-to-day form of racial harmony, if we're to live up to our greatest expectations as a mass multiracial democracy. If there ever is to be some meaningful, working, day-to-day racial harmony in this country, it'll come out of the deep South first. And I don't think this is any accident.

FROST: How do you mean?

MORRIS: It involves a common past, a common heritage, common suffering together. It's the sort of thing that you find in the best of the works of William Faulkner. Largely a common suffering of two peoples who have lived in great proximity for years and years, and who've grown to understand each other.

Here we are now, sixteen years after the great watershed Brown decision in 1954, and nothing happened for years and years. But the United States Supreme Court last fall handed down their Alexander decision, which meant in effect massive, almost overnight school integration all through the South.

Black and white kids going to school with each other, beginning to live with each other, really for the first time, in a
school building, on football fields and basketball courts.

Ralph Ellison and I gave a lecture together at Millsaps
College in Jackson recently. On a Saturday morning at eleven
o'clock I gave a speech in the old state capitol in Jackson,
in the House of Representatives chamber where the State of
Mississippi seceded from the Union in 1861, where my great-
grandfather had been a force. And got a standing ovation,
saying just what I'm saying now.

A little white kid came up to me after it was over, and he
said, "Mr. Morris, you're absolutely right." And he said, "I'm
from Carthage, Mississippi." And I remember Carthage, Mississippi, a tough little town—I played a lot of football there—
and he said, "I'm the president of the student body." And
then he corrected himself, he said, "No, I'm now the co-
president of the student body. They've merged the student
bodies, and there's a Negro president and a white president."

And he said, "We're beginning to understand each other
in a day-to-day way. And I just wish the adults would leave
us alone for a while and let us try to work it out."

FROST: Tell me, how do you feel about the quality of life
in general in America today? Do you think life today is
pleasanter than it was ten years ago, or less pleasant?

MORRIS: I think it's infinitely more tense than it was as
recently as ten or fifteen years ago. I do a certain amount
of speaking on college campuses. I believe in getting out
around the country. I think an editor of a magazine based in
New York ought to be knocked around a little.

I find it very tense right now. I think people are more concerned now about the quality of our culture in America than
at any point in my lifetime. I'm very concerned about the
strain of violence in our society now. I come from parts of
the country where we grew up with violence.

I gave a talk to David Riesman's big undergraduate course
at Harvard recently, and the only point at which I was literally hissed was when I came out against violence. And I lost

103

my temper, kind of diplomatically, the way Lyndon Johnson used to, and I said, "Well, I come from parts of America, Texas, Mississippi, and New York City, where if you talk violence long enough, you're sure to get it. And in whatever form that you ask for it."

I'm deeply concerned about this kind of rhetorical, fashionable violence that, as you know as well as I, does exist in many parts of this city, in some of the intellectual salons.

FROST: Is it in people, or is it somehow conditioned by the place?

MORRIS: Well, I think it's both. In Texas I find that violence is an almost gleeful thing. I think the South ends and the West begins at that particular place on Highway 73 in East Texas—it's right beyond the Texaco station—where the majority of the fistfights in beer joints on Saturday night begin to take place outdoors, rather than indoors. There's a passionate kind of joy in Texas violence.

In Mississippi this kind of violence is much more tense and shadowy, and brooding. Which comes out in Faulkner. I remember when I was growing up in Mississippi I knew two boys in my high school class who killed their mothers.

Violence in New York City, I think, disturbs me even more because it seems to be more coincidental, and more of an expression of what we are becoming as a people, which is a very crowded urban society. This kind of urban violence disturbs me the most, because I don't see a real cure for it.

FROST: Looking ahead, do you see us getting tenser and more violent?

MORRIS: I'm a great believer in the necessity for a powerful, dramatic, civilizing political leadership, and a presidency. And you look back—I agree with Arthur Schlesinger on this point—that we've gone through cycles in our history as a people in which we go through these periods where we get more tense, more brooding, where political reform is at a minimum on the one hand. There are cycles of reform, where the country itself seems to come out of its old brooding fears, and to express the very best in itself.

104

We are a very complicated country, America is. I love America, but I don't think we've ever fulfilled our deepest dreams as a people.

I took my son to a movie which you might have seen, on Jack Kennedy, the other day, called *Years of Lightning, Day of Drums,* which was actually put out by the USIA, I believe. It was a very moving film, an expression of the very best in us.

Jack Kennedy was one of my heroes. I actually think Bobby would have made a greater president than his brother. I thought in the last five or six months of Bobby's life, tragically short life, he was beginning to come to terms with the terrible great complexities of what we are as a people in this country. He almost had a Lincolnesque quality. You could look in his eyes and see this in the late months of his life. And I think he had a premonition, much as Lincoln did, that somebody was going to knock him off. And they sure did.

He was catching this need, this vibrancy for a leadership that bridges all of our complicated races and ethnic groups, and our regions, in America.

Right now I think we're going through a kind of low period. You might say that I'm not one of the great admirers of our current administration. Although I do agree with our Vice President that there are a lot of effete and impudent snobs on the Upper East Side of New York.

But I think that given the nature of what we are, a mass, messed-up, multiracial society, we desperately need—more than a more contained and civilized society like England— a dramatic, full-force political leadership.

FROST: Can you see anyone with the potential to do that?

MORRIS: I have a very high regard for Bill Moyers, who is not very well known in this country now. Bill was, you know, the number one man in the White House under Lyndon Johnson, and he left in 1966. Bill is an example of a young American who knows the country extremely well, who is a skilled administrator, who knows Washington, and who has a sensitivity to what this country needs, and to, I guess, the very reluctance within us to reach some degree of civilization in America.

Bill is an example. Bobby Kennedy said that if he were elected President—this was shortly before Bobby Kennedy was killed—that he would make Moyers, at the age of thirty-three, or whatever it was, thirty-two, Secretary of State. He would have made a great one, a really great one.

FROST: Would Willie Morris ever come to politics?

MORRIS: Well, there's a story about—I guess my roots are in Mississippi, David—and there's a story about this old Negro sharecropper by the name of Dan McGee, who died and went to heaven—I remembered this when I was thinking about going back into Mississippi politics—and he was escorted into the presence of the Lord, and the Lord embraced him and said, "Dan McGee, we've been watching you down there in the Mississippi delta for seventy years, and you've done the cause of human brotherhood and Christianity so much good that we're going to send you back to Mississippi to get into politics."

And Dan McGee said, "Lord, I appreciate those sentiments, but I'm not going back. You've never been to Mississippi, you don't know what it's like." And the Lord said, "Dan McGee, if necessary I'm going to put that in the form of an order." And Dan McGee said, "Well, Lord, if you send me back to go into Mississippi politics, will you go with me?" And the Lord said, "I'll go as far as Memphis."

(*Laughter and applause*)

FROST: Looking back over your years in Mississippi and your years in Texas, who's the favorite Mississippian you met, and who's the favorite Texan character that you met?

MORRIS: I guess the favorite Mississippi character that I met, and it was under unusual circumstances, was William Faulkner. He's a great hero of mine. And I was just a kid. But I'd started reading his work. And I think Faulkner was writing things in his great catastrophic fiction fifteen or twenty years ago that have become prophetic in human terms today.

And I went out on Sardis Lake with him, outside of Oxford, Mississippi, and we went around in a sailboat. He didn't say anything for two hours. So it really wasn't a conversation. He was smoking on his pipe. And finally after two hours he turned to me, and he said, "Well, Morris, anybody put any dead cats on your front porch lately?"

And I suppose the most interesting character that I've known in Texas would have to be somebody of my generation, a fellow named Bob Eckhard, who's now a Congressman from Houston. He's probably somewhat too liberal ever to be elected, say, to the U. S. Senate, or anything.

But he used to wear a great big old cowboy hat, he was a marvelous man. And I said, "Eckhard, why do you wear that dirty old hat?" And Eckhard has this thick drawl, he said, "A man with a hat like this and a drawl like mine couldn't be a liberal."

Somebody once walked up to his mother, campaigning in a supermarket in Houston, and said, "Mrs. Eckhard, we're favorably inclined toward your son, Bob, in this re-election campaign. But we're a little worried about his liberal views on the race issue." Mrs. Eckhard said, "Oh, I'm afraid that's my fault. I raised Bob to be a Christian."

(*Laughter and applause*)

Can Don Quixote Whip the Telephone Company
into Shape?

◆

Ralph Nader

FROST: If you had to point to one thing that's come out of all your campaigning, what would you pick on?

NADER: The uniform installation of seat belts and shoulder harnesses. I think that's the one most important safety feature, if it's used. Even going to the point of protecting people in many collisions up to sixty miles an hour. That is pretty significant.

FROST: You'll never really be able to protect people totally in an accident, will you? In a fast accident. Is there any danger that people could get to a point where they feel so safe in a car that they actually drive faster than they would have done before you came along?

NADER: If we get a car that is that safe, most of our worries will be at an end.

FROST: People will go around having crashes all over the place.

NADER: Modern technology can give us vehicles, in the present price range of automobiles, that will protect us against death and injury up to sixty miles an hour, and make higher speed impacts survivable. That would save thirty to thirty-five thousand lives a year. Whether people would take even greater risks, I think, is not too much of a serious worry. We have speed limits which can be enforced by police and radar, et cetera. I'm sure a few teenagers might take more chances, but you can never go on the premise that if you make something safer people will take more risks. On that theory, if you make something more dangerous, then they'll behave more safely.

FROST: No, that doesn't work, certainly. What do you feel most passionately about at the moment? What change or reform in our society would you most like to see?

NADER: Well, it's something Englishmen also object to. The growing concentration of corporate power. Take-overs, mergers, stifling out the small-business man, controlling the market, abusing the consumer, violating the antitrust laws, basically becoming more and more of a collectivist economy.

FROST: Can you give me an example of what you mean?

NADER: Oh, sure. In fact I'll put it in the most basic terms you can imagine. There was a recent price-fixing conspiracy which was successfully concluded by the Justice Department against a number of plumbing manufacturers—and the price-fixing conspiracy dealt with all the fixtures that are seen in our washrooms and bathrooms. The increase in price was estimated to cost the consumer between five hundred million and a billion dollars. That's an illegal act, a violation of the antitrust laws, and a siphoning from the consumer of that amount of money. Price fixing in this country is literally an epidemic. It's rampant. The Justice Department can't begin to have the lawyers to prosecute it successfully.

That's one example of corporate looting, which far exceeds the looting in the streets, in terms of sheer dollars and number of people affected.

FROST: As you go into all these campaigns, what are the pressures on you? Have people ever tried to buy you off?

NADER: Earlier in the campaign they would oftentimes make representations such as, "Why don't you come and join this so-called company and put some of your ideas to work?" It's done very subtly, you know. But it isn't being done any more.

FROST: What other ways do they do it?

NADER: Actually, no other ways any more. No ways at all. I think General Motors taught the rest of the companies of the country that lesson, at least. It just won't work now.

FROST: By putting a detective onto you. That was the biggest break you ever had, wasn't it? The fact that they put that detective onto you?

109

NADER: You may call it a break. It wasn't a very pleasant experience.

FROST: What was it like at the time? When you found out about it? Was it terrifying?

NADER: Friends would call me up and say, "Congratulations." I'd say, "For what?" They'd say, "I understand that you're being considered for a lucrative position in industry." I'd say, "Where did you get that idea?" They'd say, "Well, somebody called me up and wanted to interview me, as a background." Of course the interview, which was basically an investigation by detectives, was engaged on the pretext that I was being considered by some unknown client for an executive position.

FROST: Really. Is your phone ever tapped?

NADER: That's hard to say. It's difficult to have adequate detection facilities. I don't worry about it at all. As far as I'm concerned, anything I say over the phone is all right for the country to hear.

FROST: So you don't know. Obviously you haven't heard voices saying, "Ralph talking again, Frank" or anything like that?

NADER: I've heard a lot of voices, but it's due to bad telephone service.

FROST: How good are guarantees, in general? Most goods have a guarantee on them, but it usually turns out to be meaningless.

NADER: If they run as good as the mercury that slips between the fine print, they're extremely difficult to enforce. They're basically good only to the point that the vendor decides they're good for. To give you an example, most people buy appliances or other consumer products, and if they lose out, it's a matter of ten to fifty dollars. The dealer and the manufacturer know that no lawyer is going to take a case of that small amount. And they base their policies on that knowledge. These small consumer complaints are outside the legal system. And this holds true for automobiles as well. You know the so-called lemon, which is proliferating these days far removed from orchards.

110

People go and plunk down three, four thousand dollars for a brand-new automobile. They come back, the defects begin piling up. And I get hundreds of letters every week on these kinds of defects. And there's really no recourse. It just doesn't amount to much. Once in a while someone will buy an elite lemon, like an Imperial, a Cadillac, or a Lincoln, and the problem will be four or five thousand dollars. He can go to a lawyer and it's worth the lawyer's time. But not the run-of-the-mill defects, which can't be corrected.

But some consumers are really imaginative. One, for example, painted lemons all over his car and said, "This lemon can be obtained at ———," and he named the dealer. He drove it all over town.

FROST: That's very imaginative. But you're right. I mean, most guarantees are not worth taking legal action over. As a child we used to buy some chocolate bars in England that cost threepence, and there was a very impressive guarantee on the back of these things: "If the purchaser finds any fault with the excellent chocolate bar contained within, he can post the wrapper back to our works in Yorkshire somewhere, a replacement bar will be sent." But it cost fourpence to send the wrapper back. So they were terribly safe with their cast-iron guarantee.

NADER: There also needs to be much more disclosure of contents to people. You get a more complete list of ingredients in dog and cat food than you do on food for human consumption. Literally.

FROST: I've heard of a person who eats cat food all the time, and I know that a lot of people eat dog food, but one of your main worries at the moment is baby food, isn't it?

NADER: Yes. Here's an illustration. The leading companies in the industry are putting monosodium glutamate in baby food. That's to enhance the flavor, so to speak. They're putting in salt and sugar. But for whose taste? For the benefit of the mother, because the infant does not have taste discrimination. But if the mother likes the taste she will purchase the product and feed it to the infant.

It just so happens that not only do these ingredients cost

more, but they have no nutritional value. And they may be potentially harmful, particularly to infants who have hypertension tendencies, as they develop in later life. And they don't need them at all.

Do you know how easy it would be to have these baby-food manufacturers delete these ingredients from baby food? All it would take would be about three or four thousand letters from mothers around the country saying in no uncertain terms that they do not want to purchase baby food on the basis of how it tastes to them. But they want to purchase baby food on the basis of how nutritious it is for the infant. And it would change.

The consumers have a voice, they really have a part, if they will only speak up. You've got to develop a consumer power organized around things like the food industry, automobiles, insurance, telephone services, all these industries, in order to develop the voice of the consumer.

FROST: You said consumer power. As the years have gone by, you've been proved right, again and again. But you've also got more and more power yourself. Power to influence, at least. Does it ever worry you that power will corrupt you in any way?

NADER: No. Because it doesn't amount to a whit. It just amounts to talking. You tell people their frankfurters are filled with fat up to thirty-five or forty percent; you tell them that their appliances are wearing out; tell them the cars are coming out with more average defects—thirty-two per car in tested cars by *Consumer Reports* last year. You tell them that—

FROST: Thirty-two defects per car?

NADER: Thirty-two defects per car. You tell them that there are illegal interest charges all over the country, being charged, and they're concerned. But they don't do much about it. They're pretty complacent. They just sit and watch television.

FROST: Which has thirty-two defects per hour.

(*Laughter and applause*)

Is the Mafia a Threat to National Security?

◆

Ramsey Clark

FROST: There have been many things in the news that began or happened during your period as Attorney General, lots of them connected with both Martin Luther King and James Earl Ray. There are so many different accounts of who asked whom to tap whom on that whole business. What exactly was the sequence of events?

CLARK: I don't know. That happened apparently, if it happened, beginning probably in 1963. That's the earliest date that's officially in the record. And within three years of that there was absolutely no wiretapping or bugging of Dr. Martin Luther King at the federal level authorized in any way while I was in office, which began about October 1, 1966. What happened before that, I don't know.

FROST: At whose instigation, in your judgment, did it take place at all?

CLARK: Well, I worked in the Department of Justice for eight years, and I never knew an Attorney General to instigate a bug or a wiretap. I've known that department since I was pretty young. I remember walking down the corridors there when I was nine years old with my father, and it's not reality to think that an Attorney General gets this close to investigative particulars.

So, it would be most unusual to think that it was initiated or instigated. These things come to an Attorney General, who makes a judgment and he decides. What came to Bob Kennedy and what judgment he made, I don't know. I do think one of the most sensitive and touching statements that I've heard were the words of Bob Kennedy when he was advised of the death of Martin Luther King, and there's no question in my mind but what Bob Kennedy thought Dr. King was a very great man, as do I.

FROST: And so that all the balance of certainty in your mind is that Robert Kennedy did not instigate that.

CLARK: Well, in terms of instigation, that would be my judgment, yes. As I said earlier, it's an unhappy thing to talk about. I believe in the Department of Justice. I gave a good part of my life to it, and I'd like to give more to it. It's a great place and an institution devoted to justice. Its people are devoted to justice. So, I hate to be in apparent conflict there.

But as I said, the FBI asked me to tap or bug Dr. King as close as two days before his murder, and I consistently refused to do so.

FROST: In fact, you never said yes to any bugging, did you?

CLARK: In the domestic area, there was no authorized wiretap or bugging after October 1, 1966, to my certain knowledge. When I say in the domestic area, I mean as far as domestic types of crimes are concerned, organized crime, or any of the other types of domestic crimes. The wiretapping that was authorized was exclusively in what we call the national security area. This means foreign nationals. It means foreign governments. The theory is that a nation can protect its citizens from conduct within its borders. By definition it has to if it's effective at all.

But by the same definition, it cannot protect itself from activities outside its borders, and therefore, for generations it's been the practice of modern nations to engage in very intensive intelligence operations. They want to know as much as they can possibly know about what others are doing.

And unhappily we live in a world where wiretapping has been rather extensively utilized by all foreign powers in this way.

FROST: But since in the internal area you didn't authorize

114

any wiretapping, where does that fit in with that mysterious statement that Attorney General Mitchell made, that there are five hidden microphones currently in use, far fewer than just before President Nixon took office?

Does that mean that there was bugging going on that no-body told you about?

CLARK: I don't think so. I tell you, I think the two sentences that you've taken from his statement were not in sequence. I think the "far fewer" that he was referring to was not five bugs. I think it was the total wiretapping. He said he took off a number in the national security field because he found them unproductive. Of course they're unproductive. It's one of the most wasteful investigative techniques that man has yet devised.

FROST: What?

CLARK: Bugging. Bugging and wiretapping, too, you know.

FROST: Why are they wasteful?

CLARK: Because they take a lot of manpower. Frank Hogan, the very distinguished and, I think, one of the most effective district attorneys in the United States, in New York County here, has testified it takes two to six men to man one wiretap. Now, two to six investigators can do a lot of investigation. When you look back through the fifties, when the use of wiretap and bugging was uninhibited in law enforcement in New York City, you find that they weren't claiming forty to sixty convictions to result from wiretaps in any year, when thirty, forty, fifty thousand criminal matters had to be disposed of and were disposed of by the courts each year. Forty to sixty convictions.

To secure those convictions, they would have two to three times that many wiretaps on, with two to six men sitting there twenty-four hours a day listening, hoping that somebody would say something on the phone he shouldn't say. It's just not efficient.

FROST: Does somebody listen all the time, or does it go into a tape recorder and people occasionally listen to the tape recorder, or what?

115

CLARK: Well, historically the practice has been live monitoring, and the theory is that something might happen that has a time urgency about it. You can imagine what it means to professionalism in law enforcement, sitting in some crummy little hotel room or in some squad room in the back end and listening to nothing, mostly, of course, because usually there's nothing going on.

I have seen logs of all the sound that transpired in a room over a period of many, many months contain absolutely no evidence of any crime or any evidence that led to any crime, federal, state, or local. An immense waste, a demoralizing sort of thing, an immoral sort of thing.

FROST: Immoral in what sense?

CLARK: Well, immoral in the sense that government has to be fair. Government has to concede the dignity of its citizens. If government can't protect its citizens with fairness, we're in real trouble, aren't we? And it's always ironic to me that those who urge wiretapping strongest won't give more money for police salaries to bring real professionalism and real excellence to law enforcement, which is so essential to our safety.

They want an easy way, they want a cheap way. They want a way that demeans the integrity of the individual, of all of our citizens. We can't overlook the capabilities of our technology. We can destroy privacy, we really can. We have techniques now—and we're only on the threshold of discovery—that can penetrate brick walls three feet thick.

FROST: How? What sorts of things?

CLARK: You can take a laser beam and you put it on a resonant surface within the room, and you can pick up any vibration in that room, any sound within that room, from half a mile away.

FROST: I think that's terrifying.

CLARK: You know, we can do it with sound and lights, in other words, visual-audio invasion of privacy is possible, and if we really worked at it with the technology that we have, in a few years we could destroy privacy as we know it.

116

Privacy is pretty hard to retain anyway in a mass society, a highly urbanized society, and if we don't build and discipline ourselves now to traditions of privacy and to traditions of the integrity of the individual, we can have a generation of youngsters quite soon that won't know what it meant because it wasn't here when they came.

FROST: You're really saying that Big Brother could be watching us in any society now because of the technology.

CLARK: It's not that government's evil. It's that it's doing this and we come to accept it, and it grows and masters us, like television itself, if you excuse the reference. What do we know about the meaning of seventy million television sets on three- and four- and five-year-old kids that were born with the set in the room? It was there before they were. I was an adult before I ever saw television, and I've got some perspective about it.

But if I were born in a time when there was equipment in the room that recorded all the sound and images in there, it might not ever occur to me that this is a very peculiar thing, why should there be a screen or whatever it might be—it could be a pinpoint with the technological capabilities that we have—in this room that records all the sound and all the sight and puts it in a computer, and somebody that wants to, five, ten years from now, can look at everything. They can look at everything I've said or done in that room over this period of time. This is something that we really have to protect ourselves against. And it's got to be done now.

FROST: Concerning organized crime, do you feel that we are winning the battle against the Mafia and other crime syndicates, making no progress, or losing ground with it?

CLARK: Well, that's a pretty big question. Let me say first that it is a real thing. A lot of people think organized crime doesn't exist. It does. On the other hand, a lot of people think it's the total crime problem. Far from it.

Organized crime doesn't need to exist. President Johnson's crime commission in its survey of seventy-one cities only found nineteen where there was any significant presence of

117

organized crime. Among five cities of between two hundred thousand and a million people surveyed in 1967, only one was found to have a significant presence of organized crime. We don't need to have it.

What did we have in the twenties? How can we compare it with the sixties? I think if we knew, we would find that the presence particularly of that segment of the organized crime that's known as La Cosa Nostra, the Mafia, was a much more significant part of the total crime picture in the United States then than today.

When forty men are wiped out in gun battles on September 11, 1930, you have to wonder how much worse things have gotten today. Are we soft now, or what is it that these things don't happen any more?

So, it depends on your time frame. We can eliminate organized crime. That's one of the happy battles. It's not like street crime. It's not like ordinary crime. But you're not going to eliminate it with a wiretap technique or something like that.

FROST: You said in a conference we were both at in California that organized crime is different from other crime in the sense that it thrives on giving people what they want in one way or another.

CLARK: That's right. Organized crime deals in goods and services that people want. People don't want to be mugged, you know, or have their car stolen or their bank robbed or something like that, but they want to gamble, and they want money badly enough to pay any rate of interest, and they want narcotics and stimulants and depressants, and they'll pay money for them, although they know they're illegal, and they want prostitution and things like that. Organized crime deals in goods and services that people want.

The Wickersham Commission told us in 1931, and President Johnson's commission in 1967, that organized crime cannot flourish without at least the neutralization and probably some substantial corruption of the processes of criminal justice generally at the local level. How else can it? You know, if

118

there are hundreds of people out there that are gambling, law enforcement knows about it. You can't not know about it.

You or I could go to any city in the United States, and we could just show a little roll of money and say, "Where's the action?" and if there's any action around there, we'd find it, because they're looking for us, just like we'd be looking for them.

How Do You Justify the Church's Stand on Birth Control?

◆

Fulton J. Sheen

FROST: If someone came to you in confession and said he was a devout believer, but that on grounds of conscience he felt there was nothing wrong in using contraceptives, let's say the pill, and he intended to continue using them, what would you say?

SHEEN: If he was satisfied absolutely in his own conscience, I would assure him that he was not doing what was right. I'd assure him also of the mercy of the good Lord. But let me mention a few of the principles that would be behind that distinction.

First of all, the Holy Father in his letter, the *Humanae Vitae*, never mentioned the pill. Now what he held out for was that Eros leads to Bios—that love leads to life. If the purpose of sex is not life, then what is it? Death. He held for a continuity, and so do I, for a continuity of love and life, that there will be no deliberate, mechanical frustration of the transmission of love and life.

In the Church of St. Clement in Rome, down in the basement of it, two or three stories deep, is an altar to Mithra. It dates back a few centuries before Christ. And along the wall, the only place in Rome, is found a vomitorium. And in the cult of Mithra the people would eat the banquet, then they would tickle their throats and go over to the vomitorium and disgorge themselves.

It seems to us to be rather a contradiction of eating and

120

its purpose of nourishment. When a farmer, for example, plants seed, it just does not seem right for him, once he plants it, to dig it up. When an artist picks up a chisel and weds it to his marble, we like to see a statue. And when a writer picks up a pen and weds it to paper, we like to see prose or poetry.

FROST: But you're not suggesting that there would be issue in the case of every time that a couple made love anyway, are you?

SHEEN: No, no, no, of course not. Not any more than every time I talk I make sense.

FROST: That rather pejorative picture, comparing the use of a contraceptive to the use of a vomitorium, doesn't apply, because in a tremendous number of cases no babies result. You see, I don't see why you say that if love doesn't lead to life it leads to death.

SHEEN: Well, what does it lead to?

FROST: You were mentioning, for instance, that the aim of eating is nourishment.

SHEEN: Yes.

FROST: Now a couple who make love and don't have a baby as a result often end up tremendously physically, spiritually, and emotionally nourished.

SHEEN: Right.

FROST: With no thought of a baby.

SHEEN: I am not saying that there must be issue. After all, one of the purposes of sex in marriage is to deepen and intensify love.

In the mechanics of sex there is something that is voluntary, the making of love. There is also in the marital act something that is involuntary on the part of the man, something that is almost at a certain point automatic; something that is not his own. As if God had put into man this automation which didn't belong to him, and which was not wholly under his control.

FROST: I don't see how in the act of making love the man is any more out of control than the woman.

121

SHEEN: I'm not saying out of control—

FROST: I mean, I don't see that there is this *deus ex machina*, as it were.

SHEEN: No, certainly there is not that.

FROST: Take the act of making love of a married couple when the woman has been through her menopause. They know in making love that their act is not open to the transmission of life.

SHEEN: The point is not that the sexual act must end in an issue. The point is there must not be a mechanical frustration of the issue.

FROST: What's the difference between one woman of forty-two who's had a menopause and can't conceive and makes love, and a woman of forty-two who hasn't had a menopause and uses the pill, and therefore can't have a child? I don't see the difference.

SHEEN: The difference is a mechanical frustration.

FROST: What do you mean by frustration?

SHEEN: The mechanical interruption of love and life.

FROST: But it doesn't interrupt love or life. It may interrupt the creation of an issue, but how does it interrupt love?

SHEEN: That's what I mean.

FROST: How does it interrupt love?

SHEEN: It interrupts the natural transmission of love and life. It's very much like the farmer taking up his seed after he's planted it. Here there is the destruction of something that was planted. There is a deep sense, not just of sterility, but almost of a want of usefulness and purpose and goal, where there is a repetition of an act that doesn't end in an issue, where you have always a frustration of that act.

FROST: I don't think people feel that, do they? Do married people in the audience here feel a sense of frustration if they don't have a baby?

SHEEN: Oh, no, that's not the point.

FROST: You said if there's a repetition of an act without an issue, eventually there is frustration.

SHEEN: No, no. We're like two people talking over a back

122

fence. We're talking from different premises. I am not saying that the sexual act must end in an issue. You are contending that I do.

Let me put it in another way. Suppose all the Catholics went around blindfolded. Very soon perhaps bishops would say, "Listen, take off those blindfolds. Why did you blindfold your eyes? Take them off. Don't you know why your eyes were made?" Suppose every Catholic went around with his ears plugged? The Pope would say, "Take the plugs out." Do you know what would happen? We'd be condemned for condemning ear control, and eye control.

And simply because I would be opposed to wearing a blindfold on the eye, I would not be opposed to a man sleeping. In other words, he wouldn't have to see.

FROST: I think there's a difference, because you're introducing something completely unnatural. And I think that because you're calling things like birth control unnatural, you may be putting an unnatural block in the way of love-making.

Let me try and put it another way. On television programs, whenever I deal with this subject at all, I receive a tremendous number of letters from anguished married couples. And if the world were as simple as your exposition on this point says, then the world would be a much easier place. But the fact of the matter is that all over the world there are couples who, for one reason or another, both 1) love each other and want to give expression to that love, and 2) dare not have another child.

They dare not for one of two reasons. Maybe they've got five children already, and they can't afford another child. They know in terms of what they'd like to provide for a child they love that they cannot provide that. Or in some cases the wife has had a miscarriage, and it's mortally dangerous to her to expect another child, to have another child. And they want to give expression to their love. And in those situations they want to turn to some form of birth control.

They know that the safe period is not safe. What do you recommend to them, that they desist, cease making love?

123

SHEEN: No, no, now here you're talking—

FROST: What do they do, when they've got their three children and can't afford a fourth, when they've had a miscarriage and they daren't risk a fourth? What do you say to those people, cease from making love?

SHEEN: No.

FROST: Or use birth control?

SHEEN: No, absolutely no.

FROST: What do you say?

SHEEN: I say to them, I am still convinced that this is not right, but under the circumstances you must trust in the mercy of God. And you continue to make love.

FROST: With or without birth control?

SHEEN: With birth control.

FROST: With birth control.

SHEEN: Yes, with birth control.

RACE: EVERYBODY WINS OR
EVERYBODY LOSES

◆

THE INTEGRATION of her colored and white citizens is thought by many people to be America's most intractable problem. Some even think it is insoluble. There are both blacks and whites who will tell you that harmony is actually impossible. They say the two groups must be parted. They sound like the ancient emperor Alexander. When he was asked to solve the problem of a rope tied with the Gordian knot, which was fantastically complicated, he "unraveled" it in the most arrogant yet pessimistic way imaginable. He slashed it through with one mighty sweep of his sword.

I have had the opportunity of hearing from many Americans, black and white, making dramatic and powerful statements about the race situation. Several of them are represented here. The Congressman from Harlem, the playwright from Newark, the Senator from Arizona, the preacher from Chicago, the mayor from Cleveland, and the American prophet of doom who is now living in Istanbul—as well as one non-American guest, an African who works in America, the Ambassador from Sierra Leone.

I disagree with the pessimists among them. While America does have a serious race problem, I agree with the long-range optimism of Carl Stokes, mayor of Cleveland. He was talking about his city but he could just as well have been talking about all of America when he said that the *real* problems "just don't have a complexion. Pollution, transportation, housing, the destitute, education—these are just plain urban *problems*. They have no color to them."

What Makes a White Man Black?

◆

Adam Clayton Powell

FROST: Is Bimini integrated?

POWELL: We have one thousand eight hundred people, and forty-nine are whites.

FROST: Are you fair to your racial minority?

POWELL: We do our best to take care of you people.

FROST: Thank you. In that case it might be a nice place to visit.

POWELL: I welcome you.

FROST: Would I want to live there?

POWELL: (*Laughs*) It's called Adam's Shaggy Paradise, baby.

FROST: Tell me something. The fascinating thing about you being a spokesman for the black race is a) you don't look black, and b) you have said on various occasions that you have Cherokee Indian blood, white blood, and so on. What makes you feel black?

POWELL: When I was ten years old I met the man who founded black power, named Marcus Garvey. And I sat at his feet for two years. And he taught me that the color of your skin is not the way you think. In fact, *you* could be black if you wanted to be.

FROST: How?

POWELL: By thinking black.

FROST: And what is thinking black?

POWELL: We who think black don't want to be any better, and no less, than any other ethnic group in the United States.

(*Applause*)

127

FROST: But what do I have to do to think black, to be black?

POWELL: Just to think that a human being made in the image of God, regardless of his color, is the same as any other human being.

FROST: Well, I think that.

POWELL: All right. Then, second, you must think that in this United States of America—not quite united, by the way—that we have ethnic organizations. Polish-American Congress, B'nai B'rith, American Jewish Congress, Federation of Italian-American Organizations. And the only organization that we have, as of now, is the National Association for the Advancement of Colored People, with a white president. And the day you put a black man on the board of B'nai B'rith, or a soul sister on the board of the Polish-American Congress, then that day I say the millennium has come.

But until then we're not going to tolerate the NAACP, nor any whitey to lead us. They can follow us and be troops; they can be maybe corporals, some sergeants, some lieutenants. But no generals, baby, no generals, baby, no generals.

FROST: What about the people you lead? Do they ever resent the fact of your white blood?

POWELL: My babies in Harlem love this old daddy. I'm sixty-one years old this year. I paid my dues. Been in Harlem now sixty years. They know where I go, that I'm right.

FROST: Do you believe that there's no difference between black and white that a change of heart can't cure?

POWELL: Oh, yes, change of heart can cure anything. That I concur with one hundred percent.

FROST: So you believe that the two can come together with that change of heart, they don't have to be apart.

POWELL: They just did. When the SDS split the other day in their convention, they split because the white campus militants had joined hands with the Black Panther militants. So if those two can come together, we can come together, baby.

Is Democracy a White Man's Word?

◆

LeRoi Jones and John Akar

FROST: In your ideal America, what role would the white man play?

JONES: You mean in the affairs of black people or in his own life?

FROST: Well, in the whole country and then in the affairs of—

JONES: Well, basically we would like to see white people play three roles. One is nonintervention into the affairs of black people; secondly would be financial and resource help to re-establish a strong black people; and the third would be to liberalize their own community.

FROST: What do you mean by that?

JONES: Well, to liberalize it, to make it easier to live with. I think that not only black people in America, but perhaps people in the world, have found it a little difficult living with America at times, and what we're saying is that we would like to see the community liberalize itself.

FROST: About a year ago, I think it was, I remember putting to one of your countrymen the question, "Would you mind if your daughter wanted to marry a man not of your race?" Would it worry you if she married a white man, or would you be happy, or indifferent?

JONES: I wouldn't be happy about it, no. I don't think it's an unusual statement that I'm making. I'm sure most people want to see their own line, their own culture, continued.

FROST: You wouldn't be happy about it?

129

JONES: Not especially, no. I don't think that has a great deal to do with anything at this particular stage.

FROST: It was Governor Wallace whom I asked, in fact, and he agrees with you.

JONES: I can understand that. And I'm sure you might give the same answer if you had a daughter.

FROST: No, well, I don't have a daughter, but I don't think I would.

JONES: I'm not saying this in some spirit of repressing anything. It's just that I believe that people naturally seek out their own.

AKAR: For all this is worth, I'd like to give you my views on this.

FROST: I was just going to ask you.

AKAR: I think quite seriously that this is an old chestnut. But perhaps in the loving union of individuals lies the solution of the problems of the world. Because let's face it, races don't marry. Individuals do.

Several years ago my eldest daughter, who's very dark, came to America when she was about six or seven years old, and there was a party given for her here in New York City. A lot of the children came, and they were all colored, but varied in color from my daughter, who was one extreme, to another who was almost blond and blue-eyed.

In the course of the party, something extraordinary happened which has remained indelibly in my mind. Jackie, my daughter, kept talking about a friend of hers in Sierra Leone, "Oh, I want to go back to Freetown. I miss my friend." One of the children, only about eight, said, "Is your friend white?" And Jackie said, "Oh, I don't know, but she's English." I thought to myself how marvelous that a child didn't think in terms of color symbolisms.

But the other day, as a result of all that is going on in America and so on, I almost broke down in tears when Jackie watched a show on television. She came to me and said, "Daddy, if I married a white man, would you object?" And I spent the better part of one hour explaining to her that it did not matter at all whom she married, provided that he loved her and would care for her and would do exactly for her as her own father would do. And I think this really is the essence of a man in human relationships, because there is more to it than just the togetherness engendered by being black or being Jewish or being white. These are arbitrary and man-erected barriers which must disappear, and if they don't disappear in the mind, they will not disappear in the world.

(*Applause*)

JONES: We think that's kind of a fantasy, actually, and most of these people applauding, if they had to face that decision, would get hysterical, even though in this comfortable studio they can applaud some fantasy like that.

But more than that, what we're saying is that the minute black men, especially black men at a certain level, or black women, achieve that kind of prominence, they're so involved in a kind of white world that they take their energies, their talent, their resources, and disappear into the white world with it.

FROST: But why do you say it's fantasy? Didn't you marry a white lady yourself?

JONES: Right. And we were also divorced because it was a youthful error, just like I'm sure you've made some youthful errors. I don't know if Mr. Akar is a youth. But what we're saying is that black people themselves have to develop. We have to develop a political determination based on our ability to be together as a people, as a nation, before we can achieve anything else.

FROST: But it just seems to me that in terms of the relationship of two individuals, race ought to be irrelevant.

JONES: But it is not irrelevant because with race is contained ethos, and these are questions that you know as well as I do. James Brown and Frank Sinatra are two different quantities in the universe. They represent two different experiences of the world. It is a liberal lie to say it's irrelevant. If it was irrelevant, then it would not be a white power structure that controls America. It would be like any kind of power structure.

America is a racist country based on white control and white control over the world's resources.

FROST: But surely, democratically, there should be white control of America, shouldn't there? Democratically, if there are more whites, there should be white—

JONES: Well, democratically, which is like a Greek word and I guess an explanation of white nationalism as it began in Athens, you would have control over your slaves, definitely. But we were not here. We were brought here to do work for white people.

FROST: But don't you agree that in a democracy the majority has the right to rule, admittedly with generosity, with tolerance?

JONES: Well, we think that in Newark. But because we pushed for a black mayor, they say we're racist; yet you agree with us, that the majority should rule.

FROST: Good, you're pushing for it in Newark, and therefore, you support it in the whole country.

JONES: Right, but we say that because there—

FROST: You support that majority rule in the whole of America, do you?

JONES: There's nothing really I can do about it at this point, but we're saying just because you are a majority—

FROST: —in the whole of the country.

JONES: Don't be rude, Mr. Frost.

FROST: No, but you said, don't be—

JONES: I'm just trying to finish. Will you let me finish?

FROST: We sound like a double act here. Don't be rude, Mr. Frost. Don't be inconsistent, Mr. Jones.

JONES: No, if you would let me finish—

FROST: You can finish.

JONES: We're saying that white people, because they have slaves, made black people slaves, and took away the right of their self-determination and then tried to call it democracy, but we were brought here to do work in—just like me bring-

132

ing you into my house to have you work for me and then say I have to follow the rules of the family, you see.

It's not really a democracy. The people who are included in the democracy are the European Americans. A person of color, by the very fact that he has color, is described as a person not included in the rule and privilege of the majority.

And to try to hoodwink Negroes and other loyal slaves that somehow they are participating in this democracy is to be manifestly evil. And I think more and more black people of color are finding out that this democracy only exists for white people. You understand.

FROST: Well, if in a democracy seventy percent of the people feel one thing and thirty percent feel another, it is usual for the seventy percent's views to be given expression. You wouldn't disagree with that principle, would you?

JONES: No, I think that what we've overlooked, unfortunately for us, is the experience of slavery, which was not done democratically, so that from that failure to enter into the democratic process with us, then the whole rest of the democratic process has to be laid waste. There can be no democracy in a slave regime.

FROST: It's not a slave regime now, is it?

JONES: Well, I can't argue about that.

AKAR: I think I might slightly disagree with you, that it isn't always what a majority says is necessarily true.

FROST: All I was saying was that the phrase "white rule" in America is a misleading phrase—

JONES: It's not misleading. It's absolutely correct.

FROST: —in the sense that it is something which should be stopped.

JONES: It's absolutely correct.

FROST: Because obviously, it could be tolerant or anything else, but there will always be a white voting majority—

JONES: Well, is that percentage in the Cabinet? Is there a democratic distribution of power in the Congress? In the Senate? Is there this democratic distribution of power at any level of federal, state, local government, anywhere in America. Absolutely not.

So, it's a fantasy to talk about it. To parade certain Negroes, Sidney Poitier style—*Guess Who's Coming to Dinner*—and to say that they somehow have made it into America is just to protect your evil and to protect the fact of the kind of game you're running on people.

But many people do not believe it, know better than that, you understand? That's what we're saying. And you shouldn't use Mr. Akar to protect that, because he knows it as well as I do. He knows exactly what is happening in America.

FROST: I'm not using him to protect that. I'm using him to speak as an individual.

AKAR: Perhaps, in a nutshell, the larger issue as I see it is that perhaps American blacks should try and get greater economic self-sufficiency. I think it is in the economic sphere that they are way behind.

We have learned this in Africa. We were clamoring through Kwame Nkrumah for political independence. It was he who said, "Seek ye first the political kingdom and the rest will come to you." We sought the political kingdom and we got it, we got national anthems and flags and symbols of success, air-conditioned Rolls-Royces and so on, but at the end of the month we went to the bank to ask the European bank manager to have an overdraft, and that doesn't make sense at all.

I think in the area of the economic, I'd like to see more participation, perhaps.

JONES: Political self-determination will bring about economic self-determination.

I'm not trying to argue with you, but to tell the audience something: that neocolonialism is not the answer to our problem, either. We must be politically independent. We must be economically—

AKAR: Where does neocolonialism come in?

JONES: From Europe.

AKAR: I mean into this argument.

FROST: You can't be politically independent, can you?

JONES: Yes, you can.

FROST: Because that would mean a separate state.

JONES: You can be self-determining.

FROST: What does that mean? I mean, deciding your own laws? Deciding your own what?

JONES: Where they affect you, yes, absolutely.

FROST: But that would be chaos, wouldn't it?

JONES: Not really.

FROST: You can't have a country with different laws for different sets of people.

JONES: You have different statutes in parts of Queens than you have from Bedford-Stuyvesant. You have laws that affect the people of any given locale in America. America has one of the most decentralized ways of running a country that exists.

FROST: I could see you could do it on a statewide basis, but you couldn't do it on individuals applying a law to one person in one house and a different law to the person next door because he's of a different color. You wouldn't suggest that, would you?

JONES: No, that's not what we're talking about. We're talking about in different cities now. We're talking about cities, states. We're talking about laws, determined by the majority.

AKAR: One or two things I must confess. One is that there might be the danger that in trying to fight against racism, the group that fights against it might recoil into some sort of anti-racist racism. In other words, that you preach against segregation, against discrimination, but you utilize it as a tool, a weapon, to achieve this. And this bothers me.

135

When Whites Are Unemployed, It's Called
a Depression

◆

Jesse Jackson

FROST: What is your most precious memory of the late Martin Luther King? Is there one particular moment that you spent with him that you cherish more than any other?

JACKSON: I guess I would have to say at least two moments. One would have to be growing up in South Carolina and not expecting anything except the conditions as they were. We just accepted the fact that we were to go to the inferior schools, we were to sit in the back of the bus, we were to pass by the water fountains and act as if we were not thirsty, or go downtown to see a movie and not really see it. We had accepted our lot, and at that time the only answer was that we were academically and biologically inferior. And here began to arise a man out of the even deeper South, the cradle of the Confederacy, with a Ph.D., who was far more intelligent and articulate than his adversaries, and who fought in such a way that nobody could argue with his program for black liberation. People could only argue with the timing and how he applied his techniques. So the experience of a redefinition of myself came as a small child. Thus, I grew up in the generation that had the privilege to operate in the shadows of Dr. King.

And perhaps some of the other, more precious moments would have to do with the many staff meetings we had where he would not only lay out programs in terms of where we were going, but he had time to talk with us personally about our own futures and careers and involvements. The experiences were too great and too many to tie it down to one single experience, to say the least. But in the midst of a conversation with him when the assassin's bullet struck him down was the most traumatic moment that I've ever experienced; but other than that, it would be very difficult to tie down one particular experience.

FROST: Mrs. Coretta Scott King said she would like a fuller investigation into the person or persons responsible for the assassination of Martin Luther King. Are you convinced it was one man, James Earl Ray?

JACKSON: It just couldn't have been one man. But the reason I have not personally been so caught up in pursuing who did it, the real issue—and I think it's the way Dr. King would perhaps have dealt with it—is not *who* killed Dr. King. *What* killed Dr. King? In terms of the atmosphere, it's obvious that the plan, the man being able to escape, where they found the man, and other bits and pieces of evidence indicate that far more people were involved. So it was a broader conspiracy, but there was a certain atmosphere—there *is* a certain atmosphere—in the nation that gives sanction to ambush and assassination of people who are not in the tide of agreeing with America yum-yum and some of her policies now that are in conflict with the best interests of mankind. I mean, we look at a nation of two hundred million people, and the top 1 percent of the population controls more than 26 percent of the wealth, and the bottom 20 percent less than 5.4 percent of the wealth. A nation that would come up nine years ago with two programs—one to go to the moon and one to rid the nation of poverty—and nine years later 54 billion dollars have been spent to get two men to the moon, to get two boxes of rocks of moon dust, and only 5.7 billion dollars for forty million hungry people, twenty-eight million of whom are white. The nation is caught up in this kind of absurd contradiction, and we find that the federal budget just last year was 157 billion dollars, and 108 billion was spent for past, present, and future wars—70 percent. And only 19 billion for health, education, and welfare collectively. So a nation that's 70 percent inclined toward killing and only 12 percent inclined toward healing indeed has some real sicknesses and some major adjustments to make, and to speak out against that nation is really to speak in its best interest and for its health. But a climate is set now that when you do speak out for the nation and against its sickness, you simply fall prey to those who are so sick that they want to be quiet in the face of this atrocity.

FROST: If you think there's that sort of mood in the land, do you fear for your own life?

JACKSON: Certainly one with a wife and children has to take it into consideration. However, one cannot really significantly involve himself in this movement of human liberation unless he really comes to grips philosophically, personally, and religiously, existentially, with money, jail cells, and death. If one can get the power to move on in spite of the monetary temptations not to move on, if one can move on in spite of jail cells that are put in your path as tyranny, if one can move on in spite of the likelihood of an early death, then one stands in a position to create new power alternatives. I mean, those of us who are Christians have a real choice between following Methuselah, who lived nine hundred years about nothing, and Jesus, who died at thirty-three about something and perhaps could have lived to have been as old as Methuselah. So in one of Dr. King's last speeches, in which he spoke of the quality of life, and it's not so much how old you are but how well you've lived the life that you had a chance to live, and given the fact that so many boys are dying at eighteen, about far less than liberating people, it just does not really matter.

FROST: How old are you now?

JACKSON: I was twenty-eight last week.

FROST: How old do you think you'll live to be?

JACKSON: That's a very difficult thing to say, except, needless to say, those of us in the movement are so aware of the fact that death is almost imminent for those that persistently

138

speak out on major isues, I guess the only difference is that at one time in my life I perhaps would have projected working on a certain job twenty years, and then where I was going to work out a retirement program. And now it's day to day.

But if I lived day to day in fear, my fear would make me die a thousand deaths. And I can't spend my energy on dying. I have to spend my energy on living. So I really don't take it that much into account.

FROST: What would you say is the most frightening experience that has happened to you in your life?

JACKSON: Perhaps most frightening was the point at which I became sensitive to the black-white conflict and the absolute dominance and military power of whites and the instilled fear that blacks have developed as a part of their—

FROST: What was the moment when that happened?

JACKSON: Well, I was about five years of age and went down the street to a store. We used to play with this white fellow who owned the local store. His name was Jack. And all of us used to run in and out and buy our candy and our Mary Jane and our cookies. And he'd play with us, and his people owned the store, and he worked. So this particular day I went into the store, and I was in a big hurry, so I whistled. I said, "Jack," I said, "I got to have my candy now." I whistled. He wheeled around and drew a .45 in my face and cocked the guard and cursed and told me to never whistle at him again, that that was not my place. The store was full of black people, but nobody acted as if they heard or saw Jack. And the first thing went into my mind was, "I can't tell my parents. Because if I tell them, they probably would be killed too." Which means that psychologically, even at five years of age, a certain realization of black fear and intimidation in the face of white military suppression, the fact that my parents were subjected at a certain angle to it, and that I had to live in the face of it set a certain indelible imprint upon my mind. But it was only when I began to get closer with Dr. King personally and philosophically that I began to deal with what all black people in America face at one level or another. You just don't say certain things in the South and live. You just don't say certain things and get a chance to work. You just don't do certain things and live to be twenty-one. And when James Meredith started to march against fear in Mississippi and many people reacted by saying that it was a useless march, James Meredith was dealing with a very basic reality of black people in America living under that kind of tyranny where fear is instilled very early. And rather than coming to grips with that fear and using courage as an antidote, we live much of our lives escaping that fear.

So he was asked while in the South, "Why don't you drink the water downtown?" He said, "Because I'm not thirsty." They said, "Why don't you eat downtown?" He said, "Well, I ate before I left home." "Why don't you go to the movies?" "I'm not interested." Which are lies that come in the face of the fear. That fear usually starts at a very early age and you become so comfortable in the face of it until you walk by the water fountains, and you aren't thirsty, and you walk by the food, and you really don't get hungry because you close off that portion of your mind.

If there's anything new now, it's that we're moving up now, and we're moving up so much so until courage has told fear to get behind, and we're moving on. And so our theme song, Billy Taylor's *I Wish I Knew How It Felt to Be Free*, becomes a different kind of song than *Trouble Don't Last Always, Sometimes I Feel Like a Motherless Child* or sad and sorrowful songs that were sounding pitiful. Now there's a yearning to be free against a yearning to just survive.

FROST: Jesse, what would you say is the state of your movement now? I mean, you're carrying on with Operation Breadbasket, aren't you, and you're getting into new things as well.

JACKSON: When I grew up in the South we used to talk about how long we could work and how hard we could work without giving out. Now we talk about getting independent. For a long time, we spoke of the movement in purely moral and social terms. We thought that where we lived was a ghetto based upon a social presupposition and that we were based or judged on whether we were good or evil, moral or immoral. The fact is that what is known as the ghetto—called that by the sociologists—is really a colony that is built upon an economic prerogative rather than a social one. So blacks really are seen as economic entities, rather than moral agents. We're seen as profits or losses, assets or liabilities.

And when one looks at the structure of the colony, it is there for four very basic purposes. One, we represent the margin of profit of every major business in the nation. Economically, we have a position of power, once it's collected, that's greater, relative to the American economy, than China, Russia, or the European Common Market.

We are the chief labor base. We are called lazy often, but we know better. I mean, we make cotton king and we hold tobacco road. And hew out the sides of mountains. And we've wanted to work so bad we've shined other people's shoes and cleaned other people's houses when our own was unkept. So we know that saying that we are lazy is just a rich man's scapegoat for not really dealing with the fact of a basic redistribution of wealth that's necessary if peace is to come to the nation.

Thirdly, we have been the soldiers in the time of war, died disproportionately in every major war. But fourthly, we have been that community that has stood between white America and real true bloody revolution. What I mean is that whites who cannot compete in mainstream white America usurp the executive jobs in the area where we live. The car distributorships—white. The banks, insurance companies, the construction companies, the construction workers, the builders, the school principals, the police.

My real thought is that when we're unemployed, we're called lazy; when the whites are unemployed it's called a depression, which is the psycho-linguistics of racism.

(*Laughter*)

Now, what is beginning to happen if one watches the construction confrontations around the nation, blacks who've been

141

lazy have got a movement going and saying, "We want to work." And the whites are fighting, interestingly enough, over the right to work in the community where we live, and yet will not let us live in the community where they live. Because of the confusion, many whites think eliminating blacks will be the solution to their problems. And many blacks in response think eliminating whites will be their solution. But the real solution is the expansion of the economy at the base, where the law of supply and demand is not used to exploit people, and both groups can have a job and income, where neither will be eliminated.

FROST: I read one quote of yours where you were saying that instead of conflict between the poor black and the poor white, they should get together, and there should be a conflict between the haves and the have-nots. Can you see that happening? Can you see a sort of alliance of poor people, black and white?

JACKSON: Well, it's really happening by negation rather than affirmation. That is, we're backing into that relationship rather than going on into it because we really see it clearly. Racism as a form of skin worship, and as a sickness and a pathological anxiety for America, is so great, until the poor whites—rather than fighting for jobs or for education—fight to remain pink and fight to remain white. And therefore they cannot see an alliance with people that they feel to be inherently inferior. But because of the tremendous job shortage at the base of the economy now, they're having to come together—the poor are—in spite of themselves. We took this tour around Illinois last year and found these poor white mothers who were caught in the same bind that poor black mothers were caught in, and in that their drive to survive is stronger than their drive to be moral, ethical, or white. The survival is really melting us into a new kind of relationship.

142

If You Were a Black Man, Would You Be a Militant?

◆

Barry Goldwater

FROST: Whether you're conservative or liberal, you're a man who has always spoken out and said exactly what you thought, as you say a statesman should. I remember saying to Moshe Dayan that if he was an Arab, "I bet you'd be a member of the Al-Fatah, because you wanted to get something done."

And I suspect that if you were a black man going for greater rights and so on, you would probably be a militant, wouldn't you?

GOLDWATER: Not if "militant" means what I think it means. I would not abuse courts. I would not abuse property of other people. I would try to advance my people the way other great advances have been achieved, under men like Martin Luther King and those who have led the NAACP. The militants are hurting the black man today, and I don't like to see this. I hope that they understand what they're doing before they do damage that will not be irreparable but will be sort of road-blocking.

We're making progress in this country. I'm not overly proud of what we've done in this country for three hundred years, but I'm not ashamed either when I look at, for example, the segregation of blacks in Africa, and as I look at other countries.

We have a long way to go, and I think that in the years that I have left—and it's far more than some people hope (*Laughter*)—I'm going to see the black man living a much

143

better life with better opportunities, better education, but I don't think that it will ever come by the clenched fist and the angry mob, any more than the white man has ever gotten anyplace using these tactics.

FROST: Would you say that Martin Luther King was the black leader you respected the most?

GOLDWATER: No, I wouldn't. I didn't know him that well. I think of some of the men who have worked in the NAACP when that was not a popular thing to do, black men who worked in the South when it was almost impossible, black men who were just determined that their race would have an equal chance, and through argument before the Supreme Court, argument before the Senate and the House, they have achieved these things.

The problem I see is, if we have much more of this militant attitude, the threat of fires and bombings and roughness, that it only stiffens the back, not only of whites, but of Negroes, too, who don't like to see this.

FROST: Where would you say your philosophy differs, then, from that of George Wallace?

GOLDWATER: Well, I think it differs quite a bit. When I speak of states' rights, I don't speak of it in the vein that it would deny the Negro or the Jew or anybody any of their rights. He looks upon states' rights as meaning that. I think the Tenth Amendment, which explains states' rights, is the strongest part of our Constitution, in that it keeps government closest to the people.

George Wallace is a dedicated segregationist. I am not. And my record in my home state will prove that, and I've never done those things for political gain. I had to go to school in Virginia before I learned that there was supposed to be a difference between Jews and Negroes and the rest of the people, and I happen to be half Jewish, so I caught half hell, I guess you might say.

I wouldn't want to be compared with George Wallace, even if I were a governor.

(*Applause*)

Are We on the Edge of Civil War?

◆

James Baldwin

FROST: Where is home for you now? It's Paris more than here, isn't it?

BALDWIN: Oh, no, I left Paris a long time ago. But to the artist, home is where he can work. And there are so many things happening in this curious country that it's hard to keep ahead of events, not to say assassinations. So, from time to time I have to leave to work, and at the moment I have a flat in Istanbul.

FROST: Is it a good place to work?

BALDWIN: Yes, for me it's a great place to work. It is both in Europe and in Asia, which means it is neither Christian nor Muslim, neither white nor black.

FROST: Are you Christian or Muslim?

BALDWIN: (*Laughing*) I was born a Baptist.

FROST: It's not *that* funny!

BALDWIN: It is to me.

FROST: And what are you now?

BALDWIN: I'm trying to become a human being.

FROST: And when does one know when one's reached that stage?

BALDWIN: I don't think you ever do. You work at it, you know. You take it as it comes. You try not to tell too many lies. You try to love other people and hope that you'll be loved.

FROST: Do you feel as black now as when you were born? I mean, are you more conscious now of being black than when you were a child?

BALDWIN: I think you should ask the question of our President.

FROST: Pardon?

BALDWIN: You should ask the question of Richard Nixon, or the Attorney General.

I don't feel you're black or white, but I am a survivor in a way of—how shall I put it?—it doesn't matter how I feel, but I'm aware of what's happening in the country, and if I say, "You should ask the President how black I feel," it's another way of saying, "Ask him to look at the record achieved in this country since 1956." I'm talking about the life and death of the civil rights movement.

I may feel in some ways blacker than I felt when I was younger, but that only means that I am on occasion determined not to allow black children to live the life I've lived. I assume the will of the majority is now represented in such places as Sacramento and Albany and Washington. I know the effect on the police in this country, the—how can I put it—the morale, the authority given them by the present administration, and that acts on black people and poor people and Mexicans and all of the dissidents and all of the pariahs of the society.

FROST: Presumably you feel there has been some progress since 1956, but you used the phrase, "the life and death of the civil rights movement." Do you think the civil rights movement is dead?

BALDWIN: I feel the civil rights movement always contained within itself something self-defeating and Martin knew this finally, too. That's why he died in Memphis fighting for a raise for garbage men. In the beginning we thought that there was a way of reaching the conscience of the people of this country. We hoped there was, and I must say that we did reach several blacks and several whites.

We did everything in our power to make the American people realize that the myths they were living with were not so much destroying black people as whites. It's one of the

146

things one lives with, to have one's head broken, but it is quite another thing to be a representative of the people in whose name it is done. It is one thing to be a victim, one thing to be one of our niggers, and another thing to be one of the people who are described when we talk about "our niggers." You see what I mean?

FROST: I think I see what you mean, but go on a stage further.

BALDWIN: Well, after all, I am speaking as Jimmy Baldwin and, for this moment, as the representative of seven million [sic] black people in this country. I have not elected Nixon. I did not go to dinner with Agnew. I know a great deal about the Attorney General and yet more about the silent majority.

I am not a young man, but I'm a black American, and I know something about the crime of silence. I know what happens in San Francisco and in Chicago and in New York when one of our representatives wants to protect the morale of the police.

I know what a no-knock, stop-and-frisk law means. It means search and destroy. I know something about the history black people have endured and are still enduring in this place.

It doesn't mean I hate white people, who are much more victimized than I, but it is terrible to watch a nation lose itself.

(*Applause*)

FROST: You've got to add into that equation, haven't you, the white people who've striven in the last ten or twenty years? They may have been born with a feeling that people of another color are somehow inferior, but they have progressed from that stand in the past years.

BALDWIN: Look, I'm not talking about other blacks. That's the great trick back into which America may tumble. We're not on the edge of a racial war. We're on the edge of a civil war. Look, white people may or may not accept it, but I am

147

one of the descendants of the slave-breeding farm. I know how I got my name. It's an old English name, you know.

FROST: Very English, yes.

BALDWIN: Well, then, I don't have anything to hide. Malcolm X said that white is a state of mind, genealogically, historically. No one really knows who's white or black, and when the chips are down, it doesn't really matter. Who knows how many black people got pale enough to pass across the color line? It's a buried part of American history. So, it makes the American estimate of twenty-two million black people extremely shaky. Nobody in this country really knows who his grandfather is. No one can examine his history, which is the trouble.

FROST: What is the greatest problem we all face now?

BALDWIN: Someone told me that in California in 1848 or '49, there were something like a hundred and fifty thousand Indians, and at the turn of that particular century, there were ten thousand, and I was really astounded by this.

Martin Luther King was right when he said this nation was one of the few nations, but not the only one, which had to destroy the indigenous population in order to become a nation. But we're not a nation yet. And if you're a black cat living in this place and in this time, though you may spend your entire life knocking on the radiators, knocking on the steam pipes to get heat, trying to get protection against the rats and the roaches and all of the horrible details one lives with in the ghetto and gets used to, you also know that if oil was discovered beneath the tenement in which you are living and dying, that wealth would not belong to you.

When the Indians were driven out of wherever they were into Oklahoma, and oil was found in Oklahoma, it did not belong to the Indians.

I'm saying that to be a black person in this century, and to be relatively conscious, is to recognize to what extent the wealth and the power of the western world depend on your condition, that your condition is in some sense indispensable to that wealth and power.

White people may not know, but I know, that the South African government, of which we disapprove, is based on slave labor and it would have a difficult time existing if we did not support it. I know what happened to Castro's Cuba. What white Americans think is happening in the world and what black people must deal with day by day are very different.

I don't like it, but I understand why a black cat refuses to talk plainly to white people. I understand that one is in a situation in which war has been declared on you, and it no longer matters about the life of someone my age.

Do you really think that I'm going forever to make pleas to the lesser of two evils? Do you really think that I expect anything from Richard Nixon?

And when a country gets to such a place, that country is in trouble.

FROST: That, alas, is all we've got time for, but you said, Jimmy—

BALDWIN: I want to say one last thing. I would like to alert the American people to this fact, that they're not after me, but after you.

FROST: Well, I said you'd only have time for one sentence, but you've got to explain that a bit further.

BALDWIN: Something very important is happening in this country now, and I think for the first time the people legally white and the people legally black are beginning to understand that if they do not come together they're going to end up in the same gas oven.

FROST: Gas oven?

BALDWIN: Gas oven.

FROST: That's overstating the point, isn't it?

BALDWIN: So were the Jews in Germany told that.

FROST: But there's no parallel, surely.

BALDWIN: There is a parallel, if you were born in Harlem.

FROST: But you've never had a policy here like the one in Germany.

BALDWIN: I will tell you this, my friend, for every Sammy

149

Davis, for every Jimmy Baldwin, for every black cat you have heard of in the history of this country, there are a hundred of us dead.

I can carry you to some of the graveyards, where boys just like me, or brighter than me, more beautiful than me, perished because they were black.

FROST: But for every James Earl Ray in this country, there's ten or a hundred thousand other—

BALDWIN: I don't think we want to discuss James Earl Ray, because I don't believe—speaking in my person as Sambo—that he could have swum across the Memphis River all the way to London by himself.

Will It Be Any Different for Carl Stokes, Jr.?

◆

Carl Stokes

FROST: What's been the most exciting moment as mayor of Cleveland?

STOKES: Exciting good, or exciting bad?

FROST: One of each.

STOKES: Well, I guess the exciting bad, of course, was in Glenville on July 23, 1968, when we had the shoot-out between policemen and some revolutionaries.

Experience good, I think, would be when we saw the response of the Cleveland community to the Cleveland Now program. And it brought the suburbanite in, and little children literally from grade school, and welfare mothers, and businessmen, and athletes, and ministers, and black people, and white people—all of them together working on this Cleveland Now program.

FROST: How would you summarize the Cleveland Now program?

STOKES: It's an extraordinary effort that involved the contributing of private monies to combine with governmental monies to launch a program over and above the ordinary, usual program of our city, and reflecting millions of dollars. A hundred and seventy-seven million dollars just for eighteen months. And about a billion and a half anticipated for the next eight years.

Never before has the community contributed private funds to serve as seed money to get programs going, like day-care centers, multipurpose centers, recreation centers, job training, business training for minority group members. It just went right across the board.

It's a great demonstration of how a city can come together and work on its common problems, regardless of whether people live in the suburbs or in the central city.

FROST: Is there any hope for the central city throughout America? Are people going to continue to move out into the suburbs everywhere, and just flock out of the center of our cities?

STOKES: No, I think that your latest studies are going to demonstrate that the move to the suburbs has slowed almost to a trickle. The reason is that it's pretty well populated out there, and most cities now have some kind of program of providing housing within the city for the middle-income-class person.

And then the motivations for moving are so much less. At one time when people talked about the suburbs, they talked about green grass, and open fields, and they never thought about the costs. And the suburbs have not become the Utopia that they had thought.

In Cleveland, one of the things that was interesting but traumatic happened when we had a strike of our transit workers. We had been talking to the suburbanites about how they've got to help subsidize the transit system. "Oh, no," they said, "we don't have to do that." They felt it was Cleveland's problem.

Then one day the Cleveland Transit System workers struck. And all of a sudden three hundred and forty-eight thousand people who had had to come into the city and leave that evening found out that they *do* have a stake in this institution of Cleveland's. I think it helped to give them some insight in some of the other areas.

FROST: What's the nicest compliment you've received since you became mayor?

STOKES: I think it was probably from my little boy, who was eleven at the time. I only have a two-year term in Cleveland. And last year I really had to think seriously about whether or not to run for re-election. The first year and a half was a tough period. I never dreamed it would be like that.

So I sat down at the table with Carl, Jr., one morning. And I asked him, "Carl, do you think I ought to run again?" And he said, "Yes, I think you should." And I said, "Why?" He said, "Well, I think you've done a pretty good job."

(*Laughter and applause*)

FROST: Talking of family life, you married the same lady twice, didn't you?

STOKES: Yes!

FROST: How did that come about?

STOKES: It wasn't so difficult, because actually the double marriage was really a single marriage, in the sense that we ran off and got married secretly, and the family never knew about it. And the family, of course, wanted us to have a large wedding. So we went on with the large wedding, just as though we'd never been married.

FROST: How long in between?

STOKES: Only eight months. No divorce. And thankfully no children.

(*Laughter*)

But now we have three little guys. We've got Carl, Jr., and he's now twelve. Claudie is nine. And little Cordell, who is just a year old.

FROST: What sort of a parent are you? Are you strict?

STOKES: I'm not much of a parent, David. This is one of the greatest sacrifices that those of us in public life have to make. You see, ever since Shirley and I married, I've been running for office or been in office. I was in the legislature for five years. And then went into the mayor's office. I ran for mayor once, and then ran again before I got elected.

So for twelve years I've really been in the community, in almost any place except at home with Carl, and then Claudie, and then Cordell, as they grew up. It imposes a difficult burden on you. When I come home at night, if the kids have done something wrong I can't punish them. Because that's the only time that day the kid gets to see me. And if I punish him, then the impression develops in his mind that every time he sees Dad it's something negative, some kind of punishment.

As a consequence, the burden has been left on Shirley all these years of being Mom and Dad, and disciplinarian, and cook, and everything else. It's been tough, but she's done a great job.

FROST: Tell us about Captain Cleveland.

STOKES: Well, the Captain Cleveland show is a TV show that a young, brilliant ventriloquist came up with. He suggested using this dummy, Clem, and for me to just get into a conversation, for a children's show. It sounded a little questionable at first, but I said that I'd try it, because we wanted a chance to really talk to kids. I guess the age range of the viewers of his show is around eight years old.

So we did a show. Clem sits, like right in the middle of you and me. And the ventriloquist, John, has him talking to me, and we talk about everything. We talk about police departments, why we don't have more mounted policemen, what should a kid like him feel toward policemen. He asks me about taxes. What are taxes? Or why do people have to pay taxes? What am I doing about water pollution, for instance, he asks me. John is so good at his profession, that I get to talking to Clem, and it's just like talking to you, or—

(*Laughter*)

FROST: That's the source of the phrase that David Frost really is a dummy.

(*Laughter*)

STOKES: No, not really! But, you forget that this is an inanimate object. And we just have some delightful little conversations. And John knows how to pitch his questions in such a way that a six-, seven-, eight-, ten-year-old listening understands the question. And when it comes to you like that, you can respond to it simply.

And particularly when you feel pretty soon like you're

154

talking to your own little boy. In fact, one day I took Carl, Jr., on the show with me, and we had a three-way conversation.

We've been doing this now for over a year and a half. And I found that when we go out into the neighborhoods, the kids have seen the show. And I ask them then, what do you remember about it? And a kid will tell me, "Well, you said that in order to get more recreation centers, that our moms and dads are going to have to pay more taxes, and that you're going to keep the horses for the police."

I made a trip to Europe once, and Clem and I talked about it, and about the differences in some aspects of European and local cultures. Invariably I'll run into a young boy or girl who will tell me about it. And so we found out that it was educational, that it was worthwhile, it was making a contribution.

FROST: You mentioned water pollution. When you took office the Cuyahoga River was considered a fire hazard, wasn't it?

STOKES: It was considered just a hazard at that time. Then it did catch fire. So it's no longer just a hazard. It's a reality.

FROST: Well, what can you as the mayor do about things like that?

STOKES: Oh, we've done some things. Let's take Lake Erie first. It's the most shallow of the Great Lakes, and consequently pollution has made greater inroads than any of our other Great Lakes.

I have a young fellow by the name of Ben Stephansky, who is our Utilities Director. And he came up with the idea that we know will take a billion and a half plus dollars to implement. But, he said, let's let kids swim in the lake right now.

Well, we went out into the lake and carved out a thousand-yard stretch of it, hung curtains down into the water, weighted them on the bottom, and then turned over all that water inside to our treatment plant not far from it, and literally created a pool in the lake.

We have on the average of a thousand kids a day using that pool. Then we created one on the west side of town. The first pool that we created was at a place in Cleveland called White City Beach. And when I get re-elected we're going to change the name of that!

(*Laughter*)

Then we came up with a one-hundred-million-dollar water-pollution-control bond issue, and we took it to the public, which passed it, two-to-one. Now when you talk about a hundred million dollars for a city, you have to remember that President Nixon recommended an appropriation of a hundred fourteen million for the entire United States this last year. This shows how the people in Cleveland were concerned about Lake Erie and the Cuyahoga River.

FROST: Kenneth Gibson has recently been elected mayor in Newark. Do you think that your job as mayor is made more easy or more difficult by the fact that you're black?

STOKES: Well, a reporter called my press secretary, because he wanted to ask that question: What advice could I give Ken Gibson in the problems he will face as a black mayor? I told him that Gibson will have no problems as a black mayor. The problems he's going to have as a mayor will keep him so occupied that he won't even get to the ones that are because he's black.

(*Applause*)

FROST: One of the outstanding things about you is that one doesn't get any feeling of bitterness from you at all about the experiences you went through as a child. How did you overcome that?

STOKES: I don't know. I guess any person, any minority group, and certainly today any black person in America, has had those traumatic experiences growing up, as well as in his adult life, that are scarring. They're brutalizing in a great many ways.

I think, too, that when you have that kind of experience you understand that it is going to be rougher for you. You understand that the world and the people in it are not as right as they should be. The young black kids that I grew up with and I understood the discrimination, the prejudice.

We understood also that we had to do something about it, if we were going to make it. Now, along the way, I fell off the trail. But guys like my brother, and others, stayed with it, and ultimately I was able to get back on, and go back into school, and to continue.

But through all of this process, you understand that your way is going to be tougher. And the rougher they make it, the more determined you are that you're going to overcome.

FROST: When you say "traumatic experience," what were you thinking of?

STOKES: Well, I went to the best technical high school in the city of Cleveland. The kids came from all over the city. Although this school was in an almost totally black neighborhood at that time, the white kids came to it from the east and west sides.

But those of us who were Negro understood that the only job we'd get when we came out would be working in a foundry, whereas the white kids would go right into General Electric or any one of the other plants.

Then, in the Army, I'll never forget when we were on our way to Fort McClellan. The train pulled into Birmingham, Alabama, and they took all of the black soldiers into the back of the kitchen, and all the white soldiers were in the front. And the lady came back and she threw a handful of silver on the table.

And I said something—I don't know today what I said—but she turned and looked at me very pointedly. She said, "Boy, you're in Alabama now," and she turned around and walked out, and there was nothing else said. But I understood what that lady meant.

That's when you feel black, if that says anything.

FROST: It sure does.

STOKES: And then when I was in law school at the University of Minnesota, I was initiated into Gamma Beta Gamma law fraternity. Their initiation procedure was to have you blackballed a couple times, and then have some guys, who you knew were your friends, say that they're going to quit the fraternity if it didn't accept you.

Now when my friends did that, I felt that the blackballing was just because I was black. And I couldn't let the fraternity break up just because it had some idiots in there who weren't going to let one fellow in because he was black.

That was a particularly traumatic experience. The average guy who'd been going through that same procedure of initiation year in and year out wouldn't have reacted to it the same way.

So when I said, "I don't want this fraternity to break up because of me," they explained how they'd been doing this for decades. But to me it was a black-white experience, you see. This is the way you get scarred along the way.

But I did get initiated into the fraternity, right? I did go to the Army, and I did come back, and I did get the benefits of having been a soldier, and I was able to go to college. I never would have been able to go to college without the GI Bill of Rights.

And when I was in school the white teachers were the ones who tutored me and encouraged me about coming back to school and helped me to get adjusted. So along the way you find some balances.

And with all of the scarring, brutalizing, humiliating experiences that you go through, if you look for it, you'll find that there are some other factors that give you hope that in some way this country's going to straighten itself out on this business of black and white.

(*Applause*)

FROST: Do you have the feeling now that as Carl, Jr., grows up he will encounter fewer problems?

STOKES: Maybe. But, you see, Carl, Jr., will have less reason to feel he ought to encounter them. So he'll probably react to them at an intensity level about the same as mine.

You know, you just can't ignore it when a Carl Stokes is mayor of Cleveland, Ohio. It says something. After all, to give you an illustration of what I'm talking about, I went down to see Charles Evers inaugurated as mayor of a little town in Mississippi. I had no question that he could get elected in Mississippi, but I really had to go down there to see him get sworn in, because that's an entirely different matter.

(*Laughter*)

But I went down there, and Charles Evers got sworn in, and I stood there, and if you have a concept of where this country has been, and realize that here is an Evers getting sworn in, in Mississippi, surrounded by hundreds of people, black and white, and with the Mississippi State Troopers out there maintaining traffic while all of this is going on, then you're able to understand the difference between 1945, when I came through Birmingham, Alabama, and that little town in Mississippi in 1969. And this is what it's all about.

(*Applause*)

WOMEN IN REVOLT

◆

COMING FROM England, where all the girls *I* know are absolutely free and equal but still want the man to be the boss (which, of course, he always is), I was pretty shocked by the state of affairs in America. I had always understood that American women were the luckiest and happiest creatures on the face of the earth; that if any sex was put upon, it was the male sex, for it was the men who worked morning, noon, and moonlight to make their women, into whose hands each week the bulging pay packets were lovingly pressed, rich and prosperous and gay and free of worry and ulcers and heart attacks and prematurely grey hair.

Wrong! American women, I quickly learned, were having a terrible time. I could not open a paper or magazine without reading a chilling dispatch from the latest battlefront in the sex war.

So for the very first show I did, I asked about ten young representatives of the various movements to "liberate" American women to come to the studio and tell us all about their problems. They came in, the sweet charmers, and at once began arguing—not with *me,* who didn't mind one way or the other, but among *themselves,* very angrily—about whether they should sit *beside* me (which would show everyone they were equal to men), or *facing* me (which would show everyone they were opposed to men).

They bickered and quarreled on this point of where to sit, presumably absolutely fundamental to women's rights,

161

for forty minutes! And then they all walked out in a huff. Blaming "male supremacist" me! So I still don't know why I am wrong to believe that American women are the luckiest and happiest on the face of the earth. But I think I *do* know why American men love 'em. It's because they're just like women everywhere else—unpredictable.

But we can at least all savor of one triumph for emerging womanhood as outlined in a report from the battlefront:

WOMAN TO REPORTER: For a long time that's all anybody thought I was fit for. The whole house bit. I was okay as long as I was picking out a couch, buying a lamp, comparing swatches of material . . . well, I finally broke the shackles and I went and got myself a job, and I feel fulfilled for the first time.

REPORTER: What are you doing?

WOMAN: I'm an interior decorator.

Should Women Be Put Down?

◆

Ti-Grace Atkinson and Dr. Benjamin Spock

SPOCK: *The New York Times* said I believed women should be relegated to the home, the nursery and the church. And I don't feel that's a fair statement at all. I strenuously make the point that women should be able to have any kind of jobs they're equipped to fill.

ATKINSON: But some of your other ideas aren't really consistent with that. Do you think, for instance, if you say that women should stay in the home, and yet they should also have jobs, they're going to take a good part of their lives outside, if they're working? The men have got seniority. There are all sorts of practical problems, even from a conservative point of view.

SPOCK: I see. Of course, I think that the main point that I try to make all the time is that we ought, in our bringing up of girls, and boys also, and in their education in school and college, have the feeling that to take care of children, to bring them up right, is the most exciting and creative job in the world. I think that's true for fathers as well as it is for mothers.

ATKINSON: Well, if you believe this is so desirable, what would you think of giving men a chance at it for four thousand a year—

SPOCK: I think any man—

163

ATKINSON: —and have men brought up as women? What would you think of that? Wouldn't it be more fair?

SPOCK: Well, of course, this is where I think that any individual family that wants to distribute the job that way—

ATKINSON: You wouldn't have a family, probably.

FROST: Why would that be?

ATKINSON: But is it so desirable? I mean, you compare being a doctor and being a mother. And they're entirely two different things. It's like you think being a doctor and being a nurse is the same sort of thing. Do you think that you as a doctor, with the interest of analyzing, prescribing, and so forth, are at all in the same position as a nursemaid to children?

SPOCK: But I'd say you're prejudiced against children by saying nursemaid—

ATKINSON: I'm not prejudiced against children.

SPOCK: —nursemaid to children.

ATKINSON: I'm saying that it should be distributed equally. I'm saying that all people are basically human beings, and they shouldn't be divided into these political classes. I'm saying that it should be shared.

SPOCK: Well, I think in any individual family they can share it any way they desire.

ATKINSON: Yes, but you're still positing your two separate classes. You're saying girls should be brought up as girls, which means, in some sense, in a different way from the way boys are brought up. Why can't they both be brought up as human beings, and not as two separate classes?

SPOCK: Well, because I think they are human.

FROST: But they are different, aren't they, Ti-Grace? (*Laughter and applause*)

ATKINSON: I think that we've been used for different things. And I think that this is something that our whole society's going to have to answer for. It's a very serious problem. Two years ago when I joined the women's movement, at monthly meetings there would be, say, thirteen people. Now they

164

figure that at least five hundred thousand women are meeting all over the country.

SPOCK: I agree, the movement is swelling tremendously.

ATKINSON: Yes, but remarks like yours make women who have been sympathetic to the peace movement say, "Okay, let's go back in the home," especially in peace marches. Men on the left are no better than men on the right. As long as you have a war in Vietnam, you're going to have a peace movement. As long as you have a peace movement you're going to have men divided. They're going to be off our backs, and we can breathe and get this movement on its way.

But I think that you're making a very serious mistake, from your own interest in the peace movement. I think you have to give as much to women.

FROST: But tell me, Dr. Spock, you feel, don't you, that while you don't deny the point about equal rights, or human rights, that there is a basic difference between men and women?

ATKINSON: There's a basic difference between black and white people too: they have a skin-color difference. But if you're going to make it too political—

FROST: No, I meant temperamental.

ATKINSON: Yeah, but you said temperamental, Dr. Spock, emotional. And then I remember—it really stuck in my mind —you said that men are more mechanical and think more abstractly. You said women were more conservative, more, let's see, realistic, and more personal. Now that's a characteristic of oppressed people. That is not the characteristic of any other kind of class of people. And how you can't see that, when you say it, I don't—(*Some laughter*)

Well, you see, I don't find the suffering of people funny. And to laugh at it is a very bad mistake.

SPOCK: Well, I don't think that that's a sign of oppression or inferiority.

ATKINSON: Black people used to be very realistic. They were trying to survive. They're getting more and more realistic. And I hope the women's movement doesn't have to get quite that realistic.

FROST: But surely the point you're making is that you say people suffer more by not going along with the nature of man and the nature of woman.

SPOCK: Yes. I don't say it can't be done. I only say that I think in fewer cases there will be a happy, and an enjoyably cooperative—

ATKINSON: You said in an article that the relationship between men and women was going to be bad if people fought their role definitions. Essentially that's what you were saying, it seems to me. Now the relationship between men and women has been pretty bad for a long time. That's what the battle of the sexes is all about. But I think you're right. It's going to be very, very bad if men don't try to understand what women in increasing numbers are saying.

And to say you have to accept your destiny, and to define this destiny in very unattractive terms, is going to make things very, very bad.

SPOCK: I don't think that I said it in unfavorable terms.

ATKINSON: Well, that's because you weren't a woman reading it. I mean, it seemed favorable to you, because you're going to benefit from their oppression.

SPOCK: I don't think of it as benefitting. And I point out—

ATKINSON: Well, what do you say? You say men are the natural leaders, right? That's benefitting. I have the clipping.

SPOCK: No, no. Well, leaders in some respects. I would say when there's been a car breakdown, more often it's the man who tries to take charge of it.

ATKINSON: Yeah, but you use other examples. You talk about women's history. You talk about black history, and how it's good that we're studying that. And in referring to women's history, you said we should go over every course of study. In history we should emphasize Napoleon's mother, as well as Napoleon. Why? What are you talking about? Is that what black history is about, somebody's slave?

SPOCK: I was responding to the reporter who was saying,

166

"What do you mean, you want to bring up girls differently?"
And I said, well—

ATKINSON: But talking about women novelists and po-
etesses is a very good thing. But that's an entirely different
class from somebody's mother. I mean, women are entitled
to lives of their own too.

FROST: But they're entitled to be mothers as well, and be
proud of it, surely.

ATKINSON: Yes, but does that have to be their career?
That's what's down here.

SPOCK: No, I never said that.

ATKINSON: It is so. You're talking about women in academic fields, and you're saying that they—

FROST: Ti-Grace, what would you say is the basic difference between a man and a woman?

ATKINSON: Women are very oppressed, that's what I'd say.

FROST: No, what is the basic—

ATKINSON: We dress differently. I'm up here in a costume,
right? You ought to read Aristotle sometime on the way to
keep people slaves. He says expose their bodies and make
them vulnerable. And you have to think about it.

FROST: Do you feel that you're vulnerable, simply because
you're exposing your—

ATKINSON: I feel very vulnerable here. Of course I do. I've
got a man on each side. I've got people I don't know in the
audience. I don't know how sympathetic they are to feminism.
And as far as I'm concerned, for the women in the audience,
it's our movement. And we better be sympathetic. We have
to make it.

FROST: I mean, the point we said earlier about equal pay,
and those—

ATKINSON: Those are very conservative things, that's too
conservative.

FROST: —things, those are obviously just goals. But what
I don't understand is the way you sort of fight against motherhood and other things.

ATKINSON: But three years ago, when I was talking about

167

equal jobs, we were trying to desegregate the help-wanted ads in the *Times* and other newspapers, because the pay under "help wanted female" is one half of that under "help wanted male."

SPOCK: I think that's all wrong.

ATKINSON: Well, yeah, now. But three years ago when we picketed in front of *The New York Times*, people came up to me and said, "Are you a lesbian?" And I felt, what does that have to do with equal pay? Three years ago they were saying the same thing about equal opportunities that you're saying to me now.

The movement goes forward, you don't change, you're just the same. And it's building up, you know, worse and worse trouble for ourselves. And there isn't a country in the world now without a women's movement. It's really serious. This time we're going to make it.

FROST: What are you going to achieve? What will you have done when you make it?

ATKINSON: Probably, unfortunately, much more than I can even see now, depending on the amount of resistance. I mean, part of it, part of the movement, wouldn't have gone this far, we wouldn't have seen that marriage had to go, and some other things, if we hadn't first of all met so much resistance on job opportunities.

FROST: But your movement, apart from the area of—

ATKINSON: We've made a lot of progress on abortion. That's our biggest achievement so far. What do you think of abortion?

SPOCK: I think that should be a woman's right, if she wants an abortion. No question about that. (*Applause*)

FROST: Dr. Spock, what you said in your article and in your book is totally in opposition to a lot of what Ti-Grace has been saying. You've been very gracious, and you've been finding areas of agreement. What do you think is the basic fallacy in what Ti-Grace is saying?

SPOCK: Well, I think it's that women who are exaggeratedly rivalrous—and I'm not referring to you, because I don't know you well enough—

ATKINSON: Yeah, you said feminists are ferociously competitive, is what you said.

SPOCK: I think that this disposes them to think that what men have in the way of jobs and other habits is automatically better than what women have. And I think—

ATKINSON: No, I don't think—I don't want anything men have at this point. Including war, you know. I don't want any of that. What I do want is human respect. And this we have never gotten.

SPOCK: Well—

(*Laughter and boos*)

ATKINSON: Yeah, well? You're just going to have to get used to it, you're going to have to move. That's all. The male boos!

FROST: Listen, usually when we discuss this women disagree with you more than men.

(*Applause*)

ATKINSON: Well, I don't know of any men's movements for women. And the vast bulk of those five hundred thousand, I would say, that four hundred and ninety-nine thousand are certainly women.

FROST: But I'm talking about women in general. I'm not talking about the specific minority who are members of your movement.

ATKINSON: Well, it was thirteen women at first. I'm saying that now there are thousands and thousands and thousands. The last movement ended up with millions. I just hope that it doesn't take that long and that many people to get justice.

FROST: But what do you want in the way of justice?

ATKINSON: Well, it means the whole world changed.

FROST: What do you want, though? What do you want?

ATKINSON: Well, one thing: I want women and men both treated like human beings. Not saying "girls should be brought up like girls—after all they've got to take care of

169

the kiddies. I mean, this is going to be their role in life." Their role in life should be human beings, to have a destiny like a human being. And all the work should be divided equally among the people in society.

FROST: And does dividing the work mean that women don't have any particular responsibility to children?

ATKINSON: That's right. No more so than men do. It's society's responsibility. Besides children, you know, there's a whole youth movement, and children have been very oppressed too. And women have been used to it.

FROST: What is your definition of femininity?

ATKINSON: It has to go. What's *your* definition of femininity?

FROST: My definition of femininity is a woman enjoying all the basic things about being a woman, none of which you seem to enjoy.

ATKINSON: What basic things? I mean, you completely evaded that question. What are the basic things that she enjoys?

FROST: I would say that the basic thing about being a woman is two things. I agree with you that a woman should be free when she's on her own to—

ATKINSON: As long as she manages to be on her own.

FROST: No, when she's on her own she should be free to develop in whatever way she wants. She should be free to have whatever job she wants to do, whatever she wants. Equally an essential part of being a woman also seems to me to be complementary to a man, to enjoy pleasing a man, to enjoy being truly made love to by a man.

ATKINSON: What does that mean? What do you mean, complementary? What do you mean? That's not defining anything. What kind of role? Are you talking in terms of political roles? Now Dr. Spock here has been addressing the political issue.

FROST: It has nothing to do with political roles—

ATKINSON: Yes we are—yes we are.

FROST: —or anything else. We're talking about something more important than some daft protesting—

ATKINSON: You're damn right.

FROST: We're talking about human relations between two people.

ATKINSON: You're daft, not me.

FROST: Between men and women, and they're the most important people.

ATKINSON: Define what woman's role is. You have said "enjoying the things that woman enjoys." That's not saying anything. Like what? I mean, put your foot in it. You're walking right up to it, so say it.

(*Laughter*)

SPOCK: Can I fill in there?

FROST: Yes, Dr. Spock.

SPOCK: I think a woman's role in general, whether it's in the home, or whether it's in a job outside of the home, is to be the understanding, the personal, the sensitive, the comforting person. And I—

ATKINSON: Well, why isn't that human? I would like man to be the same way.

SPOCK: Well, it is, to a degree.

ATKINSON: I'd like them to be sensitive, and understanding. These are human characteristics. Why do you point these out as female characteristics?

SPOCK: I think that they're more female characteristics.

ATKINSON: Why?

SPOCK: Because I think it's clear throughout various civilizations that women more naturally, throughout the world, fit into—

ATKINSON: Margaret Mead's done work on that in other cultures. The Arapesh. There are certain people who do not set up these systems.

FROST: You know, it occurs to me: what both Dr. Spock and I are saying is that I think we have both got a much higher opinion of women than you have.

171

(*Applause*)

ATKINSON: Oh, come off it, oh, come off it. Well, apparently there are a great many women who increasingly disagree with you.

FROST: There's a tiny number of women who increasingly disagree.

ATKINSON: Tiny? What are you going to do when they get to be millions, like the last movement? By then you're going to say, "Now I agree that you've got to do away with men. But test-tube babies, that I'm not ready for."

FROST: The day when millions, and millions, and millions of women agree with all you say is the day when I'll learn how to squeeze toothpaste back into the tube again. It won't happen.

◆

Raquel Welch and Clare Booth Luce

FROST: Clare, you gave a speech in Chicago about the psychological hangups of the modern woman. You said that women have been faced with two revolutions. And now they don't really know what their role is. And as a result they're rather tormented.

LUCE: They're very confused about their own role now. Miss Welch isn't confused, because she's an actress. And you remember what George Jean Nathan said: "An actress is something more than a woman. An actor is something less than a man."

Her profession, as actress, was the first profession in the modern world that women broke into. Because even in Shakespeare's day women were not acceptable in the theater. And of course still in many parts of the world women aren't allowed onstage. Their entire role in life in most countries has been motherhood and wifehood. But that has all changed very, very rapidly.

FROST: Tell us about the two revolutions.

LUCE: Well, the two great revolutions were the Industrial Revolution, which began when men started to do women's work. Because the distaff—we still speak, when we speak of women, of the distaff side of the family—the distaff, or the spindle, was the very symbol of woman's profession. And toward the end of the nineteenth century, when the industrialists found the spinning spindles, they took women out of the home and into the factory. And that was the beginning of the Industrial Revolution.

173

And when they took woman out of her home into the factory, it was to do what had been historically woman's work, which was to weave. Since that time men have taken all of women's work right straight away from them. They're the cooks, they manufacture all the household articles that women once manufactured. They sew all the clothes, and sell them. They even wash the babies' diapers now.

So, the men, in business of course, in the professions, have robbed women of their great thousand-year-old position of being the industrialists of the home, you see. And this leaves women partially employed. That was the first thing.

FROST: So that upset the status quo.

LUCE: Yes, and women started going into the factories. And with the advent of two world wars, their services in the factories were in the beginning not welcomed, but became necessary. And the women have never gone back to the home.

Now you know, a very interesting fact is that the numbers of women gainfully employed in the United States is staggering. A very large part of the labor force.

WELCH: Are we kicking the men out of jobs?

LUCE: Fortunately, no.

FROST: Part Two of the revolution was what?

LUCE: Part Two of the revolution is, of course, woman's control of her own body. That is to say, contraceptive methods and the pill. The control of her own destiny in the form of being able to earn a living was her first breakthrough in the Industrial Revolution. And the second breakthrough is now that she has command of her own body.

And the consequences of this revolution are being seen all over the world. We call it a revolution in morals.

FROST: When Clare said she has control over her own body, a beautiful smile spread across Raquel's face. What were you thinking about?

WELCH: No, I was just thinking we don't have control over our own bodies. We have control over childbirth to a certain degree, but I don't think we have control over our bodies.

LUCE: Well, if you mean that women don't have control over their own emotions, I assure you men don't either.

174

WELCH: Well, that's probably true. But I don't know.

LUCE: But as far as controlling their own bodies, I think most people would agree that modern contraceptive methods have been a revolutionary discovery in this world.

WELCH: Oh, yes, I agree with that.

FROST: Why were you doubtful, then, Raquel?

WELCH: Oh, I don't know, because I feel that now that we are free of certain responsibilities for bearing children, and we can now express all the emotions that we do with our bodies sexually, we're looking there for some incredible reward, which I wonder if it's going to be forthcoming. I wonder if we're not demanding too much of that, and of release totally, without responsibility. Maybe I'm not making myself clear, but it seems to me that we're not free at all by losing the responsibility of children. We're less free.

FROST: Why?

WELCH: Because now we have . . . what is it? It's something. When you become free, then you really have to discipline yourself somehow. Somehow then your brain has to—or your feelings of propriety have to—govern you. It's no longer something from outside that you have no control over. You have to have the self-control. You can't look to sex to be the answer, the escape from everything, the way to express everything. Because it isn't. But people are looking to it as that, and I think becoming disappointed.

It's not the only way to express yourself creatively, not the only way to express your emotions. Certainly a beautiful way. But you take out procreation, and it presents a huge problem. What now? What are those things in your mind that you're really expressing and really releasing when you're going through this thing, without any care? Because there's no hangup now. You don't have to have the baby. You don't have to worry. So why are you doing that?

FROST: Do you think that's true, Clare? Do you think women are freer than Raquel says? Or do you think that they've got new problems to replace the old ones?

WELCH: I think there are really new problems that are more complex than the old ones. I'm sorry.

175

LUCE: I think she's quite right, the new problems are more complex. But freedom, whether it's a man or a woman, is always one thing. Freedom is choice. The wider your area of choice, the freer you are.

Now how you exercise that freedom is a different matter. There was a time when women weren't free to choose whether they wished to have a child. They were not free to choose whether they would go out and earn their own living, or get married to someone they didn't like, you see. I mean, the area of choice is always freedom. And the more choice, the more it is necessary to ask yourself what your real goal is in life.

Women are having a bad hangup because for centuries they've been brought up to believe that their only goal in life was marriage, and the rearing and raising of children. And it's very hard for them to shake that idea, and realize that they can choose, just as men can choose, to marry late in life, if that's what they want, to have one child, or none, or a dozen. And these choices make it necessary for them to use their minds, and say, "What is it I really want from life?"

FROST: Clare, in that Chicago speech you asked what is the best definition of love? What would you say was the best definition?

LUCE: Oh, did I give one in the speech?

FROST: Yes, you did.

LUCE: What was it?

FROST: Well, luckily I did read the speech. You said, "Friendship with desire," didn't you?

LUCE: Oh, yes, oh, yes, yes, yes. Love in my view is friendship with, if you prefer, desire, or lust, or sex.

FROST: Any of them'll do.

LUCE: But the durable component of love is friendship. Because obviously you can make love physically only if there is contact between bodies. You can love only if there is contact through love between hearts and minds. And bodies wear themselves out, and so does the desire. But what remains is the heart and the mind.

176

And this is another reason I feel it's so important that women should stop thinking of themselves as the inferior sex. Because a true love is only possible between equals. It's always been that way. There is no love between master and slave. That's a fiction of Uncle Tom's day, that the slave can really love his master, or the master really love the slave.

Because between equals there's always freedom. And so that a man and a woman who truly love must each believe that the other as a person is important, and not inferior in any way.

FROST: What would be your definition of love, Raquel?

WELCH: I think that love defies definition. I really wouldn't want to try to define it, because I think that it's such a different thing in each different situation. I do think that what she said is very valid in most instances. But I just know that a state of balance and equilibrium doesn't always exist, unfortunately. It's almost always a teeter-totter. And, you know, one person is giving more than he's taking, the other's taking more than he's giving. One person's in a better position than the other person at a different time; and then that changes. And there are all kinds of love.

FROST: As Clare said, is it friendship plus desire, and the desire can wear out and the friendship can go on?

WELCH: Yes, I think that that's probably true. Yes, I have an idea that without some kind of a friendship, or some kind of a thing more than the physical, it's not nearly as good. The lust part of it's not nearly as good either. Because the brain, the mind, and all the things that happen inside it, it's a very erogenous zone.

FROST: That's a great phrase, "The mind is an erogenous zone." Are you both confident about marriage existing at the end of this century? Do you think marriage will change, Clare?

LUCE: Oh, I think it's changing very rapidly, yes. In some states in the Union now there are definite proposals that marriage should be contractual over a period of time, like any other human engagement. And they're proposing in some

177

states that marriage contracts should automatically dissolve at periods, say, of ten years, when the children presumably are grown.

I think that the reasons for this are, first and most importantly, that ours is now a very mobile world. And people move around very fast. The old traditions, all of them, religion, all the rest of them, seem to be collapsing. One out of every three marriages today ends in a divorce.

And there is a drive now to legalize that thing, so that there'll be no more divorce trials, and no more struggles over alimony. Simply that people marry, and the union dissolves every ten years.

Now as a Catholic and a Christian, I deplore this. But this seems what is likely to happen. And another thing too, we've got to remember that the life span has been greatly lengthened, and that people now live to be eighty. Women outlive the men. In the old days, not a hundred years ago, you go into a New England graveyard and you'll see on the gravestone, over and over again, "Here lies John Jones and his first wife, Mary, and his second wife, Jean, and his third wife, Kate." A man wore out three women; of course, that was before they conquered childbirth fever.

Now women outlive men, according to statistics, by five years. So any kind of a Christian marriage, normal marriage, will probably last fifty years. And it's highly debatable how many people there are in the world who aren't sick to death of one another after twenty, no less fifty.

FROST: Do you find marriage natural, Raquel?

WELCH: Well, I think the contract of marriage is not necessary. Unless you're thinking about when you're breaking it up at least you have some protection for the children, that you're going to have a certain amount of material things divided up in order to keep head above water for the children's sake. But outside of that—

LUCE: May I interrupt? We can't have it two ways. We can't all go around saying how something must be done about the population explosion, and families must increasingly be limited in size if we're not all going to push one another into the sea. Things will be done.

Well, take my father. My father was one of eleven children, eleven children. The average American family today has three children. It will get down to two, and then down to one, eventually, in the course of twenty or thirty years.

Now, all this talk about keeping a marriage together for the sake of the children makes no sense at all where there's only one child, and women live to be eighty, and so do men. So the real facts of our existence—economic facts, the technological facts, the medical facts—are changing marriage every hour.

FROST: You say three children. Raquel, you're one below the national average right now.

WELCH: Well, I like it that way.

FROST: But you were about to say you believe marriage will continue?

WELCH: No, I just somehow don't believe that. Because I don't believe that two people can be held together by a piece of paper and a contract. I believe that they want to be together. And they think about how it would be without that person, and whether they're really going to find someone else that they will be that close with, and have shared that much understanding with.

That's what keeps you together. Not because there's a lot of trouble with a lawyer. And I suppose there are a lot of people that must happen to. But it doesn't happen with me. I stay because I want to be there. I don't care if there's a piece of paper or not. That's a formality.

KIDS IN REVOLT

◆

As I REALIZED while I was preparing a commencement address for the noble graduates of Emerson College, I am not old enough in years or wisdom to think I could offer any profound advice to America's young generation, the people who have brought about so many changes for the better in ideas and attitudes toward life in the past few years. They have shown us that authority is not necessarily sacred, that, in the words of E. Y. Harburg, no matter how high or great the throne, what sits on it is the same as your own. They have shown us that success and respectability and the status quo are not necessarily sacred either. Indeed, things have progressed so far that maybe now it's necessary to remind people of the opposite truth, too—that authority, success, respectability, and the status quo are not necessarily evil either, that there's no such thing as a clear-cut formula that is a substitute for an open mind and a fresh look at each and every situation.

I guess I feel this particularly strongly as some of the things the young generation are saying are what we tried to say in England with *That Was the Week That Was*. And that was when we realized how vital it was not to fall, as a younger generation, into the very rigidities of thought of which we were accusing the older generation.

It's vital, for instance, not to fall for the idea that violence is the only way to make people see reason, vital not to have two attitudes toward violence—against everyone else's but

181

in favor of your own. If it's immoral to drop bombs in Asia, it's no less immoral to plant bombs in New York. (Incidentally, morals aside, it is bad politics too, because public opinion often moves as much through a negative as through a positive response to events. For example, it was the negative response—the feeling of "I don't want to be any part of *that*" —to the tactics of a Bull Connor that brought over to the cause of civil rights many people who might otherwise have remained indifferent or even hostile.)

It's vital not to fall for the idea that anyone who disagrees with you must automatically be malevolent. A word in favor of Fidel Castro never made a man a Communist, as some people seemed to think a few years ago; likewise a word in favor of the police does not make a man a Fascist today.

It's vital not to fall for the idea that, just as the older generation seemed to reverence anything old, so the younger generation must worship anything new. Not everything that is new is also progressive. Thalidomide proved that. And I suspect that LSD will, too.

And most of all, perhaps, it's vital not to fall for the idea that change can be indiscriminate. We all want, and know we need, change, but in fact it has to be for something better than the status quo we hope it's going to replace. Otherwise we shall just end up with a new set of disenfranchised, a new class system, a new establishment, and a new set of injustices.

As I said, as straightforwardly as I could, to the 1970 graduating class at Emerson:

"The great question of the next few years is, of course, going to be whether people of different races and religions and political attitudes can live together. We don't know. We've proved all too well that they can die together. But we have not yet proved they can live together. That's going to need all your idealism. That's going to need all your toleration, too, because living together doesn't just mean living with Puerto Ricans and blacks. It means living with conservatives, and even college presidents too.

"The future is yours, and you've shown us that more important than fighting is what you're fighting for. More important than living is what you're living for. And you've shown politicians that more important than the fact that you're standing is what you're standing for.

"The future is yours. Make it peaceful, make it just, make it open-minded, make it tolerant and, please God, make it better."

What Do You Think the Kids Want?

◆

Chet Huntley

FROST: How do you find young people these days, and the new ways they demonstrate and participate in politics?

HUNTLEY: More and more I'm finding myself on their side in this everlasting quarrel, David. Oh, we talk a lot about our children, don't we? A lot is being written about them, and we're constantly bickering with our children, and we're criticizing them, and disavowing them, and opposing them, and sometimes physically beating them. Yet we keep producing them in unparalleled numbers, don't we?

But our kids, I think, on the whole, constitute a marvelous generation—the finest, I believe, our two countries, both Britain and the United States and perhaps the world, has ever produced.

Let's dismiss the few over here who are perhaps lost, and who display all the bad behavior. Every generation has had those. But I am absolutely confident that we have them in fewer comparative numbers today than ever before. We disavow, and criticize, and oppose our youngsters because of the way they comb their hair, and the way they dress. Well, I think we've got to go deeper than that, and look and see what's in their hearts and minds and souls, and not judge them on their exterior appearances. I am not particularly fond of Buckingham Palace either, but I think it's a marvelous institution.

These kids are putting us on a bit, too. When they draw us out and we conclude that they are lost souls, or that they're young criminals, or social miscasts, because of the way they dress, or the way they're wearing their hair, they know then very well that you and I are not thinking very deeply, and that we are leaping to false conclusions, and that we are rather hypocritical, and that we're just rather poor judges. I think that they're running a rather good litmus-paper test on us.

FROST: That's a good phrase.

HUNTLEY: David, I also believe it's quite likely that these youngsters are the finest patriots we've ever had. Now this may shock a few of the older generation. But these youngsters of ours, I believe, do genuinely care about this country. They really care about what it's going to look like, and what its status is in the world, and what our political institutions are, and how they're going to thrive and endure.

For example, these kids care about us, they care about each other, they care about their fellow man. They have heard us talking about the brotherhood of man, and they bought it. And now they're pointing to us and saying to us elders, "All right, we believe you. We believe all you've said about the brotherhood of man. Now how about you living up to the code that you've been talking about?" (*Applause*)

FROST: And you think that's why they pick on causes like Vietnam.

HUNTLEY: Absolutely. I can understand our youngsters' opposition to the war in Vietnam, because it was never debated in this country, David. It never was a public issue. It grew out there, and not a bit of attention was paid to it. And it accumulated like a small hurricane, way over the horizon, and grew, and grew, and grew. And finally when the number of American troops reached approximately five hundred and fifty thousand, then for the first time some attention was paid to it, and the debates broke out.

And if you'll recall, the very first place where the debate occurred was on the college campus with student sit-ins and teach-ins, as they were originally called. And the kids were involved. They were the ones who were going there to fight the war. And they wanted an opportunity to debate it and thrash it out publicly. But it was to no avail. And it was far too late to hold a debate then. The debate should have occurred about 1956.

FROST: Why do you think it didn't?

HUNTLEY: Vietnam was very far away, and we were under the illusion, I suppose, that we could just send a few men out there and give them the benefit of our wisdom, and hold off the Communist challenge.

We did go there in good faith. I can't criticize, really, why we went there in the first place. We did indeed go in response to a genuine appeal for help. Because these people in South Vietnam were getting their brains beaten out. And therefore I can't criticize the original decisions that were made. We wanted no territory, we wanted no trade, we wanted no treasure, we wanted no advantage of any kind.

But where it got out of hand, I am convinced now, is that we got trapped into it.

FROST: Was there one moment, do you think, when it went too far?

HUNTLEY: Yes, early in the Johnson administration, when the military convinced the President that with more men they could get a comparatively rapid decision, and it would all be over, and we'd all live happily ever after. And the President accepted this advice, and it was tragically wrong.

FROST: How can a President in a situation like that find out that advice is wrong? Just by listening to as much advice as he can find from as many different quarters, or what?

HUNTLEY: That's what the President of the United States is in for. And, I suppose, in more or less degree the chief of state of any country these days. He must listen to all this advice and ultimately make that fateful decision. And only he is going to make it. And it's not the first time that a President has made a wrong decision. And it's probably not the last. But this is the best he can do.

FROST: When you said that the young people want to see the ideals translated into practice, do you think it means that they'll change the party setup? Do you think that they will change the Republican and the Democratic parties in some way? Or do you think there might be a new party?

HUNTLEY: No, I think the youngsters' influence can be exerted to change our political structures, change public policy, change our behavior. For one thing, they have us outnumbered by about two to one.

FROST: Yes, I think that soon fifty percent of the population of this country is going to be under the age of twenty-five.

HUNTLEY: And soon they're going to be able to outvote us. Therefore the convictions of these young people, in a very few years, will carry. They're going to make the decisions, or they'll have the capacity to do so. And therefore it seems to me that they are going to make some changes, and some rather profound ones.

Are We All Pushers?

♦

Peter Fonda and Dennis Hopper

FROST: Welcome, Peter, very good to have you with us.

FONDA: I'm very happy to be here. I've watched my father now on this show, and I think, My God, if I can get that together as well as he did! I've never seen him so open on a show.

FROST: Delighted you say that.

FONDA: There's something about the way you don't say anything that just brings it right out.

(*Laughter*)

FROST: And he feels there's a silence there and must fill it in some way.

FONDA: He's a professional. He's got to keep it going.

FROST: Tell me. We've never had a chance to talk about *Easy Rider*. The film has become a sort of *cause célèbre*. Are you at all surprised by that? Or did you have a sort of germ of a thought that you were going to become a prophet—P-H-E-T, as well as P-R-O-F-I-T?

FONDA: Profit I-T, we figured, because the price was so low. Prophet the other way I wasn't so sure of. But Dennis, he knew all the way.

FROST: What do you hope people come away from *Easy Rider* thinking?

FONDA: I hope they just think. Or rather, I hope we stimulate them to question. I feel we've left them holding the bag.

I remember the phone call that I made to Dennis from

Torado. I was very insecure. Thank God Dennis answered the phone. I said, "Listen, listen to this idea, you know, these guys, they score some dope, and they sell it, and they make some money, and they split. They're going to retire to Florida, you know that gig, and maybe do something in Florida. And they get killed before they get there. They get ripped off by some duck hunters."

He says, "Yeah, right, that's perfect," you know. "That'll make a great film." I said, "Oh, whew."

FROST: Was there a reason why you made them drug pushers at the outset of the film?

FONDA: Well, it's a reason after the fact. I mean, I'll say it's after the fact, although we discussed it while we were writing the story. It's an immoral act, and illegal, dealing in narcotics. Cocaine is what we say it was, but we didn't dare identify it in the script. It could have been heroin. Whatever the worst thing is possible for anybody to think of.

And we take this money that we've earned dealing in hard and split to Florida to retire. Part of the great American dream is to make a lot of money no matter who goes down, and go and retire. So we make a moral problem for an audience. People will have to identify with us, especially when we bring Jack Nicholson in. He's such a lovable, understandable character. Kill him, where do they go? They have to go to us.

Now we're a bunch of dope pushers. So at the end, when we get killed by a couple of other guys who just don't like the way we look. You know, "Let's pull alongside there, I'm going to scare the hell out of them," you know, and pow. Well, the audience has to decide. And they can't make the decision. It's a moral impossibility for most of the people I know, or the great silent majority who will eventually see the film. They know their kids have. And the audience has to decide: how can we like dope pushers? How can we feel sorry for them at their demise? Are we the people in the truck? Do we do that? Are we so blind that we don't see ourselves pushing dope?

190

Because all the people are pushing dope. Whether they're pushing it across the camera with lies, or propaganda of any sort. Or whether they're pushing it in Wall Street, as Dennis says, where eighty percent of your energies are spent trying to cheat the government, and twenty percent trying to be creative within the market. All these things manifest. You know, the farmers who burn the potato crop to demonstrate something, whether people are starving, or dump the milk on the ground to demonstrate a rise of prices. Or what happened a while ago at Kent University.

These are all manifestations of fear, instinctual fear of hard problems. And when something occurs within the herd that has no precedent, people react violently.

FROST: And so you were really wanting people to come away from the picture torn.

FONDA: Oh, yes.

FROST: And it would be disturbing to you if they came away with a clear idea?

FONDA: It disturbed me that so many young people came away thinking, "Oh yeah, those people are free, you know, and they got everything together." And they didn't have it together. I turned to Hopper at the end of the flick, and said, "We blew it." He says, "What do you mean? We're rich, we made it, we retired in Florida." Well, we blew it.

Without explanation the people have to go out, the people who are interested, and say, "What does he mean, 'We blew it'?"

FROST: In addition to the content of the picture, what is there about the style that you think has caught people's imaginations? I mean, it's very lyrical about America.

FONDA: Well, that's Dennis as a director. He has a great style. As we were putting the story together, we discussed having a lyrical kind of a thing, utilizing rock and roll songs a bit at a time to emphasize our rides, and showing America the beautiful.

FROST: Yes, some of that journey was marvelous and beautiful.

191

Do you think the people who are afraid of the direction young people are taking today have got anything to be afraid of?

FONDA: Well, I went to the Pleasure Fair, which is here in Los Angeles.

FROST: What's that?

FONDA: This is a gathering of people who get it on in kind of a Renaissance flavor. And I was sitting having lunch with my two children and my lady, and we were dressed appropriately. I wasn't, I was more like this. But my lady had a peasant's outfit on from the time, and my children looked groovy. And this guy came up to me, and he said, "Oh, man, we're in a lot of trouble up in Berkeley," you know, "and we need arms."

And I'm at this Pleasure Fair, and this guy's hitting me up for money to buy arms, because these people there are uptight, and they're fighting one another in a reactive sense.

Well, we have a President who one hour says one thing; an hour later we announce a totally different aspect. And we have a Congress that's been unable to enact the Bill of Rights. And we have a people who remain silent. And we have a group of young people saying "Power to the people." Well, they've got that power, and that's what's happening.

And there's too much to even begin to talk about. I'm too wiped out about the past events. Not only in Indochina, but this country, the Mideast, the stock market, the whole thing.

FROST: Now let's talk with Dennis Hopper. I understand there is a deep personal family relationship between you and Mr. Fonda, on your left there. Is that correct?

HOPPER: Yes, well, Peter's father was married to my ex-wife's mother, and Peter's—Now wait, wait, I'm going the wrong way. But I'm close to it. Wait . . . Peter's father was married to my ex-wife's mother for the first time, right? But when Peter . . . I'm getting it confused.

FONDA: I'll take it.

192

HOPPER: You can take it with Marin and try to work it out from there, baby.

FONDA: I'll never get it straight with Marin. Marin is *your* daughter.

HOPPER: Give it from Brook's point of view. Brook is my ex-wife. That's the easiest.

FONDA: Yes, Brook Hayward.

HOPPER: We were married for eight years, and we have a beautiful young daughter eight years old.

FONDA: Anyway, Brook's mother was Maggie Sullavan, a great actress here. Maggie was married to my father the first time out for both, 1932, or '31, or something like that. Married nine months, hung right in there.

HOPPER: Boy, were they lucky I was married—

FONDA: My father was married to his wife's mother when his wife's father was my father's agent.

HOPPER: "It's Hollywood, da-da-da-da, Hollywood."

FONDA: My associate producer on *Easy Rider*, and my partner now, is Bill Hayward, his wife's brother, who was the son of my father's first wife and my father's agent, while she was my father's first wife. But, you know, we could have had a nice Italian family.

HOPPER: I tell you, I'm a Mick. The Micks and Italians made it together, and here we are.

FROST: That's the ending of that story?

HOPPER: Wasn't it touching? Very happy ending.

FROST: Really some tears, look at that.

HOPPER: Oh, if the audience only knew. I don't know how much more of this I can smoke.

FONDA: I'll take a hit. No, go ahead.

(*Crosstalk*)

HOPPER: It's Marlboro. Oh, Marlboro, I shouldn't say that coast to coast, should I?

FROST: Peter, are you sure you're comfortable there, because you know you can sit here.

FONDA: His horse ran away, and he's—

HOPPER: I gave you my horse.

FONDA: You did not, I don't take horse. I'm soft.

HOPPER: They shoot horse, don't they? I don't believe in any needles, babe. Needles are out. I take vitamin B occasionally, but I don't dig it. No, really, I swear to God. I think anyone who uses needles is totally insane. And marijuana is ridiculous if it isn't legal. I think heroin and cocaine should be legalized, because we don't need larger law enforcement agencies to take care of that kind of thing.

We need to be able to watch them, and have doctors, and be able to, like, take care of it the same way they do in England.

FROST: In England heroin and cocaine are illegal, and they ought to be.

HOPPER: Sure, but you go to a drugstore and buy it, if you can prove that you're an addict.

FROST: You've got to somehow absolutely destroy the traffic in heroin, surely.

HOPPER: Well, I would hope so. But if you're not going to do that, like, you're giving the underworld a tremendous amount of money by making it illegal. If a guy can prove he's an addict, let him go to a drugstore and pick it up. Then you can have a doctor and a psychiatrist there, and then you can treat the problem, and it's not an abstraction any more.

We don't need more policemen. We need to be able to take care of the people that way. We don't need them stealing that way. An addict should be able to go and get it.

FROST: It's not as available as that in England. You can't nip into a drugstore and get it.

HOPPER: Sorry. If you can prove that you're an addict.

FROST: You may know of a private drugstore.

HOPPER: I don't use it.

FROST: No, I know you don't.

HOPPER: I smoke marijuana and take LSD occasionally, though.

FROST: In England it's only someone who's unfortunate enough to have become hooked on heroin or cocaine who after going through a lot of tests can then get supplies gradually lessened and lessened hopefully to a cure.

HOPPER: Great!

FROST: But surely you've got to press with every force in the world ruthlessly to stamp out that traffic.

HOPPER: Yeah, but an addict is a sick person. Anybody that's sticking a needle in their arm is sick.

FROST: Of course they're sick.

HOPPER: Well, then, like, have doctors. Have it available for them. Don't, like, make them have to go out and steal. An addict has to get a hundred and fifty dollars a day. You know, *I* can't even afford that. You're making a criminal of him, so you're enlarging your police force to find him, arresting people. I mean, it's crazy.

FROST: Of course you've got to do something about people who are addicts. But how do you stop them becoming addicts?

HOPPER: Once you see who the addicts are, then you can start. First of all, the underworld's going to lose a lot of money. And, like, I think that's important. I don't think we should give them tax-free dollars.

FROST: But explain more how you stop people from becoming addicted in the first place.

HOPPER: First of all, you let the people see the addicts lined up at the drugstore, and you let the doctors and the psychiatrists see them. You expose them, so they're no longer criminals and no longer stealing out of your houses. Because eighty percent of our crimes in our cities are by people who are addicted and have to steal to get their addiction taken care of.

Legalize it, let us see it, let us deal with the problem when it's out in the open. Why do we keep pushing everything down, pushing everything down?

FROST: You seem to be saying something that you're not saying you're saying. Legalizing it is a different thing from providing limited supplies, available on medical prescription.

HOPPER: I said it about twice now. If a person can prove that they're addicted to heroin or any of those drugs, let them go to the drugstore and be able to purchase it. Let them see a doctor. Let them see a psychiatrist. They're sick. And, like, they're a problem to the society.

FROST: But you would make a criminal out of the pusher if heroin became available by prescription only, wouldn't you?

HOPPER: Well, if it was legalized. I see no difference between the man who pushes cocaine at the beginning of *Easy Rider* and a man on Wall Street who's involved in defense plants who takes all of his money and puts it in a Swiss bank. It's tax-free.

FROST: Dennis, you keep switching between the two definitions. You'd rather switch than fight. (*Laughter*) You say that the person who pushes heroin or cocaine should go to jail, I think.

HOPPER: The person who pushes it?

FROST: Yes.

HOPPER: No, I don't believe that any more than the man who is involved in defense plants should go to jail. I think they're both criminals.

FROST: He's not making a total bodily wreck of a man.

HOPPER: Yes, he is. He's sending people over to Indochina and to China and to Russia, wherever they're going to be sending them soon.

FROST: Metaphorically, but—

HOPPER: He's not only making a wreck of them. He's killing them personally.

FROST: Do you think that the person who pushes heroin or cocaine should be regarded as a criminal? Because I certainly do.

HOPPER: Well, I do too. But I'm saying he's no less a criminal than the other man.

FROST: But he would be a criminal.

HOPPER: Of course.

FROST: Peter, let's turn to the difficult subject of what one says to one's children. What sort of advice about life do you give your children? How have you decided to bring them up? How *are* you bringing them up?

196

FONDA: Well, that's a better question. Deciding how to bring them up is a deadly thing. You know, it's very hard to say. My six-year-old daughter picked up *Life* magazine and saw the My Lai massacre and asked me why. Today, fortunately, she doesn't know about what's happened recently with the students at Kent State and the students at Berkeley and the students all over the place, and all the other people. She's unaware of the implications of Cambodia or the elections in this country, and she does know other things. I don't try to protect her from that.

The only way I can relate to bringing her up is taking her out. That's a really depressing thought, to remove from this country the people who will run the country, who will be the country, to take them out before they're destroyed by the country.

FROST: Destroyed?

FONDA: Destroyed. Well, you know, on many levels it'll be very general and very light and very easy and nonpolitical and easy for this whole country to take on. What is my daughter going to breathe in ten years? People can go without food, if they're trained, for a certain amount of time. Maybe ninety days on sugar and water. They can go without water for five or six days. They can go without breath for four or five minutes. On what order is importance laid out? There won't be anything for her to breathe, let alone think about, whether it's a political society or whether people are shooting each other on the street or not. That's all going to happen. It's all happening right now, whether we would wish to expose it or not. That's going on in everybody's mind, left and right. The whole reactive syndrome. What's my daughter going to breathe in ten years? If she'll be able to survive this reactive syndrome within the society, this violence which we have bred, which we are conditioned to respond with and so forth, what's she going to breathe in ten years?

FROST: How about what's she going to hear in ten years from you? I mean, as compared with the way your generation

197

was brought up, how do you think she'll be brought up differently?

FONDA: Well, she's going to hear, as she hears now, that I love her. And she feels that I love her, and she sees that I love her. And she knows that I talk to her, and she knows that I want her to talk to me and that I appreciate her expression of herself, as does my son, and my wife. That's my family.

(*Applause*)

Did Spiro Agnew Have a Youth?

◆

The Vice President

FROST: Could we begin by talking about your own youth? I have read about it, but I'd be fascinated to know more. I was wondering, what is the most graphic memory you have of your own youth?

AGNEW: I think I had a very typical middle-class youth in a suburban area which was part of the city of Baltimore called Forest Park, and I remember those days as a young person we were tremendously active physically all the time, coming home from school and dropping the books and heading for what we called the field, where we would play softball or football or some other thing until exhaustion took us and nightfall came, and then going in and being ravenously hungry, which most young people are, and eating, lessons, and then to bed.

It was pretty much of a routine, but I think the difference between a young person's life in those days and today is there wasn't the awareness of the world as much as the awareness of one's immediate neighborhood and friends. I think it was because communications weren't what they are today.

FROST: Can you remember who your heroes were as a child?

AGNEW: Mostly sporting figures. People in books that you would read. The typical boy's hero, the Frank Merriwell type of thing.

FROST: Which books did you most enjoy?

AGNEW: Well, I remember one book in particular, and I tried to get my son to read it, as a matter of fact, because I came across it by accident. It was by a man named Ernest Thompson Seton, and it was called *Two Little Savages*.

It was a book about woods lore. We didn't live in the country, and it was fascinating to me because this book had all sorts of diagrams of how to construct a teepee and how to build a trap for small animals and how to build bird feeders and all that sort of thing, and it was quite good because it was done by a man who had great experience as a naturalist. Very enlightening and different.

FROST: Did your son ever read it?

AGNEW: He read it, and I don't think it quite got to him the way it did to me. He said he enjoyed it, but he didn't seem to be overly impressed with it.

FROST: Was there any advice that your father and mother gave you that you carry with you to this day? Were there wise words that burned themselves into you?

AGNEW: I can't reconstruct any given words of wisdom, but I can remember the emphasis that my father placed on the value of education and on what he called the need for application. He didn't subscribe much to the theory that people shouldn't be competitive, and he wasn't one to accept excuses for nonperformance on the basis that someone else was more able than his son was. He always would say, "If you apply yourself, you can do as well as anyone," and this was the message he got through to me, that application is a very important aspect of learning, because as you learn it seems to me that the information you accumulate in your life assists you in other learning.

You can turn more resources to new understandings as you accumulate information.

Probably the most difficult things a child has to learn are the early fundamentals of something that is totally unrelated to anything else, such as arithmetic, or the basics of English grammar, or something of the type.

FROST: *Life* magazine in their profile of you said that you have always continued the learning process by deliberately learning three new words a week.

AGNEW: I guess that is a little bit accurate. To the extent that I do try to accumulate some new knowledge each week, whether it be in vocabulary or some other thing, it is correct. People who stop learning because they assume that they have reached the ultimate expertise in their particular field really stagnate on the vine. I feel honestly that I have learned more in the past ten years of my life than in all the other years put together, because learning becomes more interesting as your life progresses.

FROST: You certainly taught me one new word. I am not even sure I can pronounce it right. "Tomentose?"

AGNEW: Tomentose.

FROST: When did you find that word?

AGNEW: Fairly recently.

FROST: It sent everybody in the nation, I think, running to their dictionaries.

What were your ambitions when you were young? Did you then think, "I would like one day to be Vice President of the United States"?

AGNEW: No. I never envisaged a political career. I went through the usual series of small-boy adulation for sports figures or someone who was high in the public eye, but not politics.

FROST: Not at all. So the law fairly early attracted you?

AGNEW: No, no. As a matter of fact, the law was a rather late attraction. In my earlier years I leaned more toward the idea of the sciences. I remember as a boy we had a three-story house, a fairly large frame dwelling, and there was an attic which was turned over to me for whatever I wanted. I would spend hours with my friends, particularly on rainy days, with a chemistry set or some sort of Erector set, and I always thought that I would turn to the sciences more than the law. As a matter of fact, I did in my early education.

But I found out I didn't particularly care for the laboratory applications of chemistry. I liked the theory and the

201

mathematics that went with it, but I didn't care for the lab work.

FROST: Were your parents strict? Did they believe spare the rod and spoil the child?

AGNEW: Neither of my parents ever struck me, but nonetheless I was quite careful of my father's reprimands. He was a very stern man, and contrary to what apparently is the popular motif of attempting to be a pal to your children, he was no pal to me. He was the authority in the family, and when he indicated he'd made a decision, I listened, and I was quite fearful of disobeying him.

FROST: Which are you as a parent, stern or a pal?

AGNEW: I am not a pal, and I am afraid I haven't been as good a parent as I might have been had I been in some other line of work than politics. It takes you away from your family quite a bit.

I suppose most people would consider me rather stern. On the other hand, I am sure that my children feel a great ease in communicating with me, and they certainly don't hold for me the awe and fear that I held for my father.

FROST: How do you believe that children should be chastised for wrongdoing? Do you hold with your father they shouldn't be struck?

AGNEW: I do. But I think they should be punished. They should be punished in a way that deprives them of something that is rather precious to them, because if a punishment causes a child to give up nothing, it is really no punishment at all.

One of my daughters, who was quite independent-minded, I might say, now has become the closest to me in communicating ability. I recall that I was quite stern and would punish her frequently because she would constantly repeat the violations of the rules.

Finally, after a year of rather difficult times in the house, because it's no fun disciplining children, and it's much easier just to give up and go along, we finally got the thing straightened out, and I think it worked out rather well for both of us.

FROST: What do you think straightened it out?

202

AGNEW: She finally decided that I wasn't going to quit attempting to create the disciplinary atmosphere that I was maintaining. She just had thought that if she persisted I'd give in, but I didn't. I just kept punishing her.

FROST: What do you mean?

AGNEW: Depriving her of her privileges and that sort of thing.

FROST: Can you remember your own—"rebellion" is too strong a word—but your own opposition to parental authority when you thought your parents were wrong?

AGNEW: Many times I thought I was terribly maligned and imposed upon, and I thought there was a conspiracy to make my life miserable. I think most children go through this. But with the coming of maturity, you understand that these things are really necessary, although I must say there are times that parents punish children that the parents are wrong and the punishment is not justified. Parents aren't perfect either. But, nevertheless, it is important that the child not lose sight of the fact that there is an underlying very strong affection and love that motivates the parents, and once the child recognizes this and accepts it the child accepts the punishment rather well, I think.

FROST: You used a big word there, the word "maturity." How does one know when maturity comes? People of fifty as well as twenty would be interested to know that.

AGNEW: I don't know. I guess it is a subjective judgment. There are some people who think they have reached maturity and others think they haven't. Where there are great departures in ideology and belief among people, there are always accusations of immaturity that pass between them, and it is a subjective index. I suppose it depends upon the compatibility of people with other people, whether they think they are mature or not.

FROST: When do you think you achieved maturity, Mr. Agnew?

AGNEW: Very late, I would say. I didn't really feel that I had reached any direction until I came out of the service after World War II.

FROST: Did your feelings about maturity have anything to do with your decision not to let your daughter Kim wear a black armband?

AGNEW: I think the principal consideration was that I asked her what she knew of the war and how it came about and its history. I found out she knew absolutely nothing about it. I then attempted to explain how the war had come about, going all the way back to the Japanese occupation of French Indochina, and then the Japanese leaving, and what happened as the North Vietnamese undertook their long program to take over the entire area.

She admitted the logic of my argument, but she said, "But why do they have to be there?"

And I said, "Well, Kim, you obviously didn't listen to what I said."

She said, "No, but we ought to bring them home anyhow."

Well, I felt this was not a judgment of an eighteen- or nineteen-year-old person. I think she was thirteen or fourteen then, and I just decided I wouldn't let her participate because I didn't think she knew enough about the conclusion she was reaching.

FROST: But she would probably still have liked to wear the armband, wouldn't she?

AGNEW: With any child that age, there is a great desire to go along with peer groups.

FROST: What does she feel now? Do you still have the family debates?

AGNEW: Oh, yes. She is probably my greatest contestant in the debates, and we talk very frequently. We agree on some things, we disagree on others.

I think I modified some of her opinions, and I think she has been successful in modifying a few of mine.

FROST: Can you think of something wherein she or one of your children has modified your point of view?

AGNEW: Yes. The thing that she has brought out mostly is that there is a way that people can draw closer to one another that is not necessarily related simply to logical argu-

204

ment, that there is an emotional rapport between people that solves problems that pure argument may never even touch. I have learned that from these discussions with her and seeing how deeply she feels some of these things, that she may not be able to think through step by step, but still has utter conviction.

◆

COMPARED WITH Europe, where the main topic of political debate is the Common Market—a subject which increasingly defies any attempt to deal with it without sending the entire public to sleep—politics in America seem to be much more *about* something. So many issues are still in the balance. On so many more topics, the verdict simply isn't in yet.

Not that this is an ideal situation. On the most tragic issue of all—will political agitation turn to violence?—we all wish we knew the answer. Maybe that was why Cesar Chavez was received so warmly at the Little Theatre (this was *before* his movement's greatest triumph) when in answer to my question, "Some leaders today have their doubts about nonviolence; do you still believe in nonviolence as much as you did?" he said, "Oh sure. We think that this is the real true way of struggling because, see, one of the important things is that when victory comes, if it can come through nonviolence—and I think it will—then you have retained your own worth and in other words, you're your own master. You don't have to compromise."

Men of good will struggle on, bemused at times by the toughness of the struggle. As Senator Muskie said to me, "Of course, all of us who are at my age in life—and I hope I'm not too old yet—look back to a time when Americans almost instinctively reacted to other Americans with confidence and trust. Not that we didn't recognize human weaknesses, because we did. But if one moved into a new community, one

207

expected that after a short time one would be accepted in the community, to live as though one had lived in the town for years, and we had that feeling about each other all across America.

"President Nixon once spoke of what he described as the spirit of Apollo. I think that if there is a spirit of Apollo it means this to me above all else: to see those two Americans walking on the surface of the moon was a demonstration of the capacity of the human will and intelligence to triumph over physical obstacles that ten years ago were considered insurmountable. I hope that that demonstration convinces us here in America that it is possible for us to deal with the problems that divide us against each other in the same way and to heal them and to create that feeling of unity and oneness that most of us associate with the years of our childhood and with the promise of America."

In the pages ahead, a Minority Leader in the House of Representatives, three Senators, the Vice President, the Congressman from Harlem we met earlier, and an author take a look—sometimes a hard look—at the promise of America. Perhaps we should fortify ourselves with a comment from John Akar. I asked him on one occasion about his view of the future of democracy as a system of government, as compared with others throughout the world.

"Democracy," said the Ambassador, "is rather like sex. When it's good, it's very, very good. And when it's bad, it's still pretty good."

Should Advertising Men "Sell" Politicians, and If So, for How Much?

◆

Joe McGinniss and Gerald Ford

FROST: Mr. McGinniss, your book, *The Selling of the President 1968,* has caused a great deal of comment. How did you come to have access to this whole campaign?

McGINNISS: A stroke of good luck. In the beginning, actually, the book was supposed to be about both Nixon and Humphrey together. I was going to compare and contrast their advertising styles and their uses of advertising and image-building and television. However, when I went to the Humphrey people with this idea they said, "Are you crazy? Do you think we're going to let you see what we're doing to advertise our candidate? This is private business." But, when I called the Nixon people, none of whom I knew, I said, "Who's in charge of your advertising?" and they told me. And I went to see all of the advertising people, and they all said, "We think this is a fine idea." The only stipulation they made was that I not print anything until after election day. Since I wasn't going to be in a position to start writing until after election day, that was no problem.

FROST: Now they're saying, "We meant after election day 1972."

McGINNISS: Perhaps.

FROST: Of all the things you discovered, which of the tactics surprised or interested you most?

McGINNISS: What interested me the most was the way that these advertising men, these television experts, could first have convinced Nixon himself to rely almost totally upon television

209

to get elected. Because if you think back to 1960 and 1962, if there was one medium that was unfriendly to Richard Nixon, even more than the press, it was television. Not because of any hostility on the part of broadcasters, but because of his own inability to function before a television camera. Somehow in six years he looked inside himself and figured that if he was going to come back, he was going to have to come back through TV. And they told him then that what he was going to have to do was develop qualities of personality, or, if not develop them himself, at least allow them to project qualities of personality that the American people wanted in a President. His advertising director listed among these warmth, humor, a sense of compassion, things which I think even Mr. Nixon's friends would not list chief among his virtues. He's in his middle fifties, and it's a little late for a man to change his character. So he allowed them to make it appear as if he had changed his character simply through sophisticated technical uses of television.

A brief example. He projects a cold image. And this is the way people responded to him, so his advertising director said, "One thing we'll never do is put him all by himself in front of a TV camera, just sitting behind a desk talking. This is a very cold way to deal with people. Always have him in situations talking to other people so we can take pictures of him communicating. Having an interpersonal relationship. Giving and taking. Listening, nodding, patting on the arm, you know, responding with warmth, humanity." And the advertising director wrote in a memorandum to Nixon in November of 1967 that these situations should look unstaged even if they're not. And then, they proceeded to go to New Hampshire and stage some very unstaged situations.

Another example. They talked about how he needed a sense of humor. American people want their President to be able to crack a joke or at least a smile once in a while. Well, Nixon kept his sense of humor pretty well disguised from people for a long time, including much of his own staff. Finally they turned to a man by the name of Paul Keyes, the chief writer for the *Laugh-In* show. And they hired him on a sort of retainer basis to occasionally contribute humorous lines that Nixon could use in interpersonal relationships.

FORD: I'm not an expert in this business, but it's been my observation that television really reveals the personal qualities that a person has. Having known the President for twenty-one years, fairly intimately, I happen to think that basically he has a good sense of humor. Now this isn't revealed in his business activities—that is, the affairs of government—but if the three of us were sitting in some out-of-the-way place just conversing and we were all good friends, I think you'd find that he basically has a good sense of humor.

What I'm trying to say is that all the technical expertise of the television industry can't make a person something that he isn't basically. In this case, the President of the United States has these qualities, which the technicians were able to bring out and portray.

FROST: What you're saying is that here you had someone with a sense of humor who, by being nervous or something on television, tended to lose it. The technicians were merely bringing back something that was already there.

FORD: Absolutely. In other words, that characteristic was there, and through the media of the experts they were able to bring it out in the campaign.

McGINNISS: I think I'd like to draw one distinction. Television ultimately does reveal a man for what he is, if you're talking about this kind of television where the cameras aren't in your employ. Where you don't hire the cameraman and the technicians and stage the situation yourself. Here you come on and the cameras are neutral. They're simply transmitting. They're simply allowing you to communicate, but what I think Richard Nixon did with his television cameras was stage situations which were specifically designed to bring out personality qualities which even his own advisors believed he did not have. The men who worked most closely with him in the image field, I think, would disagree with you, and from listening to their conversations over a period of twelve months they did disagree with you about these qualities of Nixon's. Raymond Price, who was a *New York Herald Tribune* editorial writer, now a White House speech writer, said in 1967, in a memorandum to Mr. Nixon, "It's not what's there that counts, it's what's projected, and we must be very clear on this point, that the response is to the image, not the man, and that this response often depends more on the medium and its use than it does on the candidate himself." Now this is Nixon's own man. This is not my accusation.

FORD: Well, I'm not saying that you shouldn't put your best foot forward. I'm simply saying that what they tried to do was to bring out the inherent qualities and characteristics.

McGINNISS: I really don't feel my book is totally an anti-Nixon book. It's more of an anti-process book. I think that there were some dishonest things done with Nixon. There are some differences between the man and the image, and we never got a chance to vote for or against the man, but only for the image. I don't think this is unique. I don't think Richard Nixon is the first politician who has ever thought of doing this.

FROST: It seems to me that a lot of this sort of advertising-agency type of thinking on the one hand underestimates the voter and on the other hand underestimates the subject of the advertiser.

McGINNISS: I think that's very true.

FROST: In this case it was Richard Nixon, but on another occasion it might be some other candidate. Do you believe that this sort of thing can work? That the voter is influenced? Do you really believe that this technique influences more than one or two voters?

McGINNISS: I really do. The people who are voting for President are the same people who are making *Mayberry RFD* and *Petticoat Junction* and shows like this top-rated shows in the country. Again it was a Nixon man who wrote in a memorandum that voters are basically lazy and uninterested in making an effort to understand what we're talking about, therefore we have to reach them through their emotions. What they want are certain personality qualities which they find pleasant and attractive. I think certainly it's unfair to the voter to cater to this taste, and it's unfair to the candidate, if he is a candidate of any substance, to present him in such a bland and ambiguous way that his real self can never get through to the people.

FORD: David, I would quite violently disagree with the assumption that the American people aren't smarter than some of the propaganda people tend to believe. I have a great deal of faith in the ultimate good judgment of the American people, and I don't think they're going to be fooled by Madison Avenue advertising techniques.

I've traveled in forty-nine of the fifty states in the last four and a half years, all over the country, and the American people really have a better understanding of the issues than Madison Avenue gives them credit for. They have a deeper concern about what's going on in the country and around the world. And despite their emotional reaction, they're interested in the issues and the problems and the people who are running the government. I don't think they're going to be fooled by any propaganda, whether it's in the newspapers, on radio, or on television. Maybe I'm a little naïve about this, but the American people are not going to be sold a wrong bill of goods by some sophisticated propaganda technique of a Madison Avenue advertising agency. They just aren't going to have that selling job done to them.

McGINNISS: I think they already have. I'm not trying to be flippant, but I really believe that all the people got to vote for or against last year was the televised image of Nixon. I think through the entire campaign he kept the whole country on the other side of the television screen. He would not allow himself to be questioned by professional questioners, only under circumstances where his own people would pay for an hour. They would pick the panel themselves, and then they would put him up live and say, "Here's Nixon answering Americans' questions." They were the questions of the Ameri-

213

cans that his own television advisors picked. I don't think this is a very legitimate way to do business. They made a big deal the last night of the campaign with a two-hour telethon. "Call up and ask Richard Nixon a question," they said, but all of the questions asked Richard Nixon on the telethon were written by members of the Nixon staff.

Ford: I think you make a fundamental mistake assuming that the American people on the last night of a campaign are going to make a final decision. Maybe the propaganda people, who are putting on the television show, thought they were. But, I have a lot more faith in the ultimate good judgment of the American people than to let them be sold by a propaganda operation the last night of an election. It just doesn't operate that way. If we ever get to the position in this country where through such techniques we're going to pick a President, then I think something's wrong with our system. I don't think it's going to degenerate to that position.

McGinniss: I think there is a lot of evidence to indicate it already has.

Is It Patriotic to Want to Pull Out of Vietnam?

◆

George McGovern

FROST: Senator McGovern, you come right from that area that the administration says supports Nixon's policies. Is your picture of Middle America the same as President Nixon's? Do you believe that the people believe the things that President Nixon believes they believe?

McGOVERN: Well, let me say I got elected in that part of the country on a rather different platform.

(*Laughter and applause*)

The President talks a lot about the silent majority. What puzzles me about it is the seeming assurance on the part of the President that he knows what silent people are thinking.

(*Laughter*)

I find it rather difficult to know what silence means. During my last campaign I took a much different set of issues to the people of my state than the President is now offering. I don't question his sincerity in the course that he's now following, but I think, for example, the American people are overwhelmingly in favor of a very, very early end to the war in Vietnam.

(*Applause*)

I don't know how President Nixon interprets his election in November in 1968, but I believe that what happened is that a set of political forces began to operate in this country more sharply after the Tet offensive in early 1968 than before, which led President Johnson to the conclusion that he should not be a candidate for re-election. I think it explains the success of Senator McCarthy in New Hampshire and after. I think it explains the great appeal that the late Robert Kennedy had. In addition, there was a feeling that somehow we were on the wrong track in the way that we were conducting public business here at home. We're spending too much money on the weapons of death, on military matters, and not enough on making life better for people to live.

FROST: Can you give some specifics, especially concerning the power of the military-industrial complex?

McGOVERN: Let me try to put it in terms of statistics that are meaningful. I think you can tell a lot about a family or a man or even a country if you can see how each spends its money. If you can study the budget, you get some index of what their hopes and their aspirations are, or even what they're afraid of, and it disturbs me that this magnificent country of ours is now devoting about seventy percent of its federal budget to war—past wars, present wars, preparation for future wars—and only about twelve percent of that budget to the whole range of programs that have to do with the quality of life—education, health, housing, the cleaning up of our water and air, all of those things that make up a more decent country. This is what disturbs me.

FROST: If you could pick one piece of legislation that you think is more urgent than any other to improve the quality of people's lives, what would you pick?

McGOVERN: A program to rebuild the cities of America, a comprehensive plan to improve the housing, the schools, the transportation system, to deal with the problems of pollution. I think this would be it. If you want me to be more specific and narrow it to one issue, I suppose, the effort that many of us have been talking about to deal with environmental problems—the pollution of our air and water. Perhaps that's the legislation I would most like to see enacted.

FROST: If you could gaze into the future, who would you say is likely to be the next Democratic President of the United States, and when?

(*Laughter*)

216

McGOVERN: Well, I guess if we've learned anything in 1968 it's that the future's unpredictable. Looking back over the way nominations have been made in the past, it's very hazardous to see what would happen in '72.

I suppose, however, we see some of the central contenders emerging. I would think at this point that perhaps Senator Muskie of Maine is a likely and strong contender. And I don't entirely rule out Senator Edward Kennedy. I know that he has taken himself out of the picture, and I have no idea what the public will think in the long run about the difficulties he has had. I suppose former Vice President Humphrey is a possibility. Senator Harris and Senator Hughes are others that have been mentioned. All of this leads me to the conclusion that it's very hard to pick out any one that might emerge as the nominee.

FROST: And you didn't mention the sixth. Senator George McGovern of South Dakota.

(*Applause*)

McGOVERN: Well, I'm going to be honest. I'm thinking about it.

(*Laughter*)

FROST: When you started running in the last campaign, you were concerned about healing of divisions in the country. Do you feel that we have progressed in that direction?

McGOVERN: I think the healing process has been set back by this administration, and I regret it very much. I think President Nixon had an opportunity early this year when he was talking about bringing us together, and talking about lowering our voices, to accomplish some healing. I don't see where we've moved very far down that road. To talk about lowering voices and then to give us Mr. Agnew, who calls people in the peace movement "impudent snobs" and "rotten apples" and that sort of thing, is very disturbing.

It seems to me, Mr. Frost, that what is under way in this country is a systematic effort to broaden the divisions, to set what you referred to a while ago as Middle America against the young people in this country. There is also the so-called

217

Southern strategy, which seeks to exploit the prejudices of human beings, to set off blacks against whites, and an effort to play off the so-called intellectuals on one hand against the main body of people. All of those things seem to me to be divisive.

I think that the attack that the Vice President made on the networks because he didn't like the way they treated the President's speech on Vietnam, his attack on Averell Harriman, one of the most distinguished Americans—all of these things serve to divide us. They create a climate of fear and tension instead of healing.

FROST: The word that comes up a lot is "patriotism." But there are differences in the way that word is defined. How would you define it?

McGOVERN: I think patriotism is the dedication of one's conscience and one's convictions to what he believes to be in the national interest. If that means calling the country away from a mistaken war, then the patriot has the obligation to speak out. I participated in the peace efforts in Washington, because I thought it was the patriotic thing to do. When one sees his country following a course that he thinks is mistaken, and not in the national interest, then to be patriotic he ought to say so—he ought to speak out, he ought to sound the alarm, and try to call the country to a higher standard, to lift the flag to a higher standard. That, to me, is patriotism.

Is Barry Goldwater a Liberal?

◆

Barry Goldwater

FROST: Who is your favorite political figure in all history? Do you have one?

GOLDWATER: That's a difficult question to answer, and I'm not answering it because you happen to be English. I think Winston Churchill is probably going to go down in history as the greatest statesman of this hundred years.

FROST: I'm delighted. What do you think makes a great statesman?

GOLDWATER: I think honesty and understanding of people and problems, a willingness to talk about problems and to lay it on the line. That was the greatness of Winston Churchill, and I think as time goes on, it's going to prove to be the greatness of Harry Truman.

You don't write the history of a President in the immediate past. You wait a hundred years before you decide if he's good or bad, but I think in the case of Winston Churchill, I'd have to—because of what he did with England when you folks really had your tail in a crack over there, and—

FROST: That's a great phrase.

GOLDWATER: In the West it means a certain thing.

FROST: Yes. Listen, I'm not from the West, but I understand that phrase. It's more descriptive than "up the creek," as they probably say in England. Which is worse, tail in a crack or up the creek?

GOLDWATER: Well, it depends on the situation. You can get your tail out of a crack, but it's hard to get down from that creek.

219

(*Laughter*)

FROST: We sometimes ask show business people who come on if they agree with that great song of Noel Coward about not putting your daughter on the stage. With all your experience as a politician, did you want your son to become a politician, too? Do you think it's a good profession for young people?

GOLDWATER: I do. I think it's a good idea for everybody to be involved in what's going on in their country and their home town and their state. He called me at two o'clock one morning and asked me what I thought about him doing it, and I started to tell him, and he said, "Never mind. I've already decided."

I thought the other son would become the politician, because this son was so successful as a businessman I didn't think he'd want to take the cut in pay. But I'm very proud of him. He's doing a good job.

And it's run in the family. My grandfather was in politics. By the way, he married an Englishwoman in London. He was a Polish Jew, and he came to this country and never quite learned the language. But he was the mayor of a small town in Arizona, and my uncle founded the Democratic Party in the territory of Arizona and was vice-president of the constitutional convention. And I'm in politics. One son's in politics, and I have three grandsons living in Texas. Now, if I can get them out of that mess . . .

(*Laughter*)

FROST: Obviously, politics is very hard work. How often have you had to do things in politics that you wish you didn't have to do? How often have you had to be nice to someone you'd love to say "Go away" to?

GOLDWATER: Not too often. It's about like your business. You have to do some things you don't like in politics like anything else. I don't think politics is a great deal different than being in business. I was a businessman myself. You try to find the answers to people's problems. You don't try to fool them.

I think the demands on a politician's social life are what

we dislike the most, because if we wanted to accept every invitation in Washington, I could average two dinners a night, 365 days a year. But I have a wife that I don't get to see enough of, and I like to spend my evenings with her. So, I turn invitations down. That gets hard sometimes.

FROST: One of the other tremendously demanding things about politics is the criticism. Are you thick- or thin-skinned?

GOLDWATER: I believe in what old President Truman said: "If you can't stand the heat, get out of the kitchen." And I think I'm pretty thick-skinned. No one could have gone through what I did in '64 and come out of it without an elephant hide.

(*Laughter*)

And I'm not mad at anybody. You learn to take it, and you learn to dish it out, too.

FROST: Right.

GOLDWATER: Once people know that you can dish it out, then they don't bother you.

FROST: When was the time in '64, though, when you most thought: When I see him again, I'll say something.

GOLDWATER: You mean, to President Johnson?

FROST: Well, maybe. I don't know.

GOLDWATER: In politics, people don't get mad at each other. Once in a while it can get personal and vindictive, but I've found some of my best friends are in the so-called liberal camp. We would never vote together, but we see each other, play golf together, entertain each other. So, you have to learn not to let ideologies, philosophies, and differences upset you.

FROST: You're known as the ultimate conservative in America. How would you define the basic difference between a conservative and a liberal? For instance, what's the difference between the two approaches to the ghettos?

GOLDWATER: First of all, the two words are almost meaningless today. When history is written, long after I'm dead, I will be called a liberal in the framework of Thomas Jefferson's liberalism or a Bob La Follette's or a Robert Taft's. Taft was called a conservative but was actually more of a true liberal.

My philosophy of the conservative is to make our progress on the proven values of the past. Now, the so-called liberal today—frankly, their camp is in a shambles, and I hope they can come out of it with something a little more meaningful.

FROST: I thought you were going to say, "I hope they stay that way."

GOLDWATER: No, no. We need the two dialogues. You can't have a one-concept government. You have to have differences, so that out of the two will come the best path.

The conservative approach, say, to the ghettos, is that we really don't know the answer. We're working at it. George Romney is working hard at it. We don't think the entire answer is a new building. We think that a lot of the answer is in the educating of the person who's going to live in that building, to respect the building, to love it and treat it as a home. This is a problem.

We don't know how to overcome this yet. The liberal, as he's done for the last thirty-five years, would merely say, "Here's X numbers of hundreds of millions or billions of dollars. This is what we're going to do."

I'm writing a book at the present time, and I'm trying to develop a chapter that would answer that question. I lived and worked in New York back in Depression days. It hasn't changed any. They keep building the buildings higher. You might be better off here someday, just clearing the whole place off and starting over again.

(*Applause*)

Now I wouldn't say that's a conservative approach.

FROST: That's pretty liberal.

GOLDWATER: But I would say, as we look at these large Eastern cities and the accumulated mistakes of two hundred years, antiquated ordinances, laws, and concepts of government, this might not be a bad idea. We might get to the day when business will be done in underground establishments, not underground, but beneath the surface, and the people live above the surface, and we have transportation not by automobiles but by automated vehicles that travel on overhead rails.

We in the West are looking at the troubles of the East and trying to prevent our cities from accumulating these same troubles.

So, while I don't offer that as an answer, I think that my home town of Phoenix will never get in the shape New York is in, even though we'll be the fifth or sixth largest city in the country by the year 2000.

You'll find a difference in different parts of our country. There's parts of our country where there's still a feeling that man does really have a responsibility to build his own hospitals, build his own churches, take care of his neighbor, and go out of his way to call on a sick person.

FROST: Where would you say in America that feeling is most strong?

GOLDWATER: You'll find it in every state in the Union. Mostly in the smaller places. Smaller towns in New York, smaller towns in Jersey. I think it probably prevails more in the West, because the West is younger, and we haven't yet reached the stage where you ignore the man standing next to you at the bar. In New York, if you offer to buy him a drink, you usually get a cold, fishy look, and "What kind of a queer are you?" Out West it's a little different.

The best night I've ever seen in New York was the night the lights went out. I was here.

FROST: Were you?

GOLDWATER: Yes. And I never enjoyed New York so much in my life. People were decent, they were nice. A guy gave me a candle to climb twenty-five flights of stairs. In Rockefeller Center. And by the time I got back down—they had a bar on almost every floor—I didn't get back home until five in the morning. And I really enjoyed New York. I think you ought to put the lights out about once a week.

(*Applause*)

FROST: You've had some marvelous experiences in your life, haven't you? Somebody was telling me a story about you when you were once briefly jailed. Was that in your student days?

GOLDWATER: I wasn't a student, no. This was before I was married. Two friends and I escorted a young lady across the Mexican border for breakfast. In those days they drank beer out of old Hills Brothers coffee cans. My leg was in a cast, and I used a cane. One friend thought it would be very nice to throw a can of beer on me. At seven in the morning. So I threw a pot of mustard at him and hit a policeman. It was the wrong thing to do.

So they escorted us down to the jail. And they let the young lady go. My two friends pushed the guard over the curb and ran, and crawled through the sewer to get back into the United States, and left me. I sat there all day. I had been stationed, in the Army, at a camp just below the border, so I started calling for the C.O., and they'd come down and look at me, and say, "No, never saw him."

So finally, about time the sun was going down, I wrote them out a check, and signed the name of one of the other fellows who ditched me. The poor fellow's dead now, but to his dying day he had that check framed, up on his wall.

You can get in jail in Mexico pretty easy.

FROST: Can you? They'll arrange it for you just like that?

GOLDWATER: Right now.

FROST: Part of the tour. Do you still fly a plane?

GOLDWATER: Yes, I fly every time I get a chance. In fact, just a few months ago I was allowed to fly the SR-71 at eighty-one thousand feet and twenty-one hundred miles an hour. I enjoy it. I'm not going to give it up till the doctor tells me I have to. Then I'm going to get a new doctor.

FROST: Do you still operate the ham radio?

GOLDWATER: Yes. I have an amateur radio station in my car, and in my apartment in Washington. At home we have twenty-five volunteers who have run forty-five thousand patches with families all over this country from their sons, and husbands, and friends in Vietnam. These volunteers are mostly retired people. I even took a slow-scan television concept to Vietnam when I went, and we transmitted pictures from Arizona to Vietnam, and back, on what we call slow-scan. It's something relatively new.

FROST: What's the oddest conversation you've ever had on your radio?

GOLDWATER: The oddest didn't happen with me. The oddest happened one night when Sergeant Nugent called from Vietnam for the Texas White House. And it took a long time to get through the Secret Service, because they'd never heard of a phone patch, and they'd never heard of military affiliate radio service, and they thought somebody was merely pulling their leg. So they finally got—I don't know whether it was Lady Bird or Lynda Bird who's married to Sergeant Nugent—but they had a conversation.

FROST: It's not Lady Bird! It's Lucy Bird.

GOLDWATER: It's one of the little birds.

(Laughter)

It just so happened that the next man in line at the Vietnam station was named Johnson, a Sergeant Johnson. I'll tell you, it sure screwed things up in Texas. The Secret Service told my operator, "You can't talk to Mr. Johnson." My operator said, "Look, I don't want to talk to the President, Mr. Johnson wants to talk to somebody in Pennsylvania. Will you get off the line so we can get through?"

(Laughter)

That's one of the oddest, although we have had many unusual things. I helped a young couple who were trying to sail to Hawaii, who got lost and ran out of rations. I got the Coast Guard directed to them.

I participated once in getting some iron lungs to a remote village in the Argentine, to help a German doctor down there who was a ham.

This is not a hobby, it's really more of a service. In fact, we have a little book that, if somebody on a ship wants to cut an appendix out, we can read him instructions. I don't

225

know that they'd try it. But we get doctors to come over and get on the microphone and say, "Now, what are the symptoms? Well, here's what I would do." So there are many interesting things go on in this field.

FROST: As you say, you're going to go on living for a long while yet. But how would you like to be remembered by people?

GOLDWATER: In a kindly way.

What's an Intellectual Like You Doing in a Race Like This?

◆

Eugene McCarthy

FROST: You say that one of the reasons you decided to give up running as a Senator from Minnesota is somewhat private. Do you have in fact private ambitions to do something quite different?

McCARTHY: It's not so much what you're really running for as what you're running away from, sometimes.

(*Laughter*)

FROST: I'm not sure I understand.

McCARTHY: Before I had gotten into the presidential race, I had more or less decided that this would be my last term in the Senate. That was the private part of it. I'm not sure whether it's a good idea for people to stay in the Senate twenty-four, thirty, or thirty-six years.

FROST: For what reason?

McCARTHY: I don't mean to fault those who do stay, but I thought that in my case it was better to leave. I left the House after I'd been there ten years, and spent twelve years in the Senate. There're some changes taking place, I think, in the manner in which you deal with problems in America. When I went to the House, the real problems were legislative —to pass certain laws that needed to be passed. In the Senate, the question's been more one of how power's brought to bear—not really through the legislative process but outside of it, for example, in confirmations, treaties, and the rejection of treaties. I'm not sure now but what you can have more influence by coming at some of these problems from outside either the Senate or the House.

FROST: You studied for a year at one stage to be a monk, didn't you?

MCCARTHY: Approximately.

FROST: Is it possible to be as moral in politics as when you're being a monk?

MCCARTHY: Well, that's a question of how moral monks are, I think.

(*Laughter*)

They have to live in a relative world too, and it's somewhat different from that of politics. The motto of the Benedictine order is, "Keep death daily before your eyes"—which is a very good motto for politicians.

(*Laughter*)

It gives you a certain freedom that you wouldn't otherwise have—if you accept it. I mean a kind of political death. And then one can take some chances along the way.

FROST: You're not planning to go back to being a monk again?

MCCARTHY: There're scarcely any monasteries left now. This is one of the changes that's taken place along the way. No, I don't really have that in mind.

FROST: Is it possible, in fact, for a politician to tell the truth, the whole truth, and nothing but the truth?

(*Laughter*)

I don't mean that politicians are dishonest as a breed, but is the whole truth just too inconvenient and impossible?

MCCARTHY: It depends on what you really mean by the whole truth. I think you can tell the whole truth. I don't know that you can tell all the truth.

(*Laughter*)

I think that in the last campaign that I pretty much stated what I thought about issues and told the whole truth. And you can do it.

FROST: But you don't get elected.

MCCARTHY: Well, I didn't get elected President, but we

228

did all right, I think. And it wasn't a question, really, of the truth-telling that made the difference.

FROST: Well, someone said that in the last resort the reason that you didn't get the nomination was that within you there was a feeling that you were fearful of being President, that you didn't want to be President. Did you want to be President or were you fearful?

McCARTHY: I don't think I was fearful. It was not really a question of fear. It's not a question of whether you want to be President. It's a question of whether you're willing to be. I said I was willing to be, and that's as far as anyone should go. I've been always worried about candidates who said that they had decided they wanted to be President when they were fourteen years old.

(*Laughter*)

Or the first time they saw the White House they said, "That's where I'm going."

(*Laughter*)

It ought to kind of happen to you along the way, I think, for the Presidency particularly. You could decide you wanted to be a Senator when you're fourteen and make a hard run at it. It's not so bad. I don't know whether those who decide that early turn out very well, but the Presidency is another matter. You ought to let it build up around you. Maybe no one else will run, or the issues are such that you must run. I was willing last year, and those who say that I say that I wasn't—well, you know, for someone who's unwilling to have it, it was a long run from January until the middle of August.

FROST: You said on one occasion you were the best-informed man in the Senate. If you're leaving it, who'll take over the title?

McCARTHY: I don't think I said that.

FROST: You were quoted as saying it. You didn't?

McCARTHY: No, I didn't. I never said that—about the Senate. I think I might have said that I was the best-informed—

FROST: Best-informed man in the world?

McCARTHY: Now, come on.

(*Laughter*)

I couldn't say that about the Senate. You're not supposed to do that with reference to the Senate, anyway. The theory is that they're like the vestal virgins—all of equal virtue. And equal intelligence and incorruptible.

(*Laughter*)

Who Is the Only American—Black or White—Who Doesn't Give a Damn?

◆

Adam Clayton Powell

FROST: You've been described many ways by many people.

POWELL: Really, really?

(*Laughter*)

Got to research that.

FROST: How would you describe yourself? Who are you?

POWELL: I am probably the only living American, black or white, who just doesn't give a damn.

(*Applause*)

FROST: About anything?

POWELL: No. About the establishment, about our society, about our sickness, about our Vietnam War, about what they're doing to emasculate the programs I put through Congress, like the war on poverty, minimum wage, equal pay for equal work. That's it.

FROST: You said that passionately.

POWELL: Oh, I thought it was objective.

FROST: No. Passionately. Now how do you answer people who say, "Well in that case, why don't you stay here and work for these things, rather than spending so much time in Bimini?" Do you feel you can work better from there, or what?

POWELL: Don't be jealous.

FROST: If there are any episodes in your stormy life that you'd like to rewrite, what would you pick?

POWELL: I wouldn't change anything. In fact I would try to live a little bit better.

FROST: What do you mean by living better?

POWELL: Enjoying the better things of life.

FROST: You said that like an old movie villain.

(Laughter)

What are the better things of life?

POWELL: Not to have what you need, but to have the creature comforts.

FROST: What to you are the creature comforts?

POWELL: Not to worry about anything. To know that your life is secure for the rest of your life, and your loved ones are taken care of. That's all any man can expect in life. What value is money, if you're not taking care of your future and the future of your loved ones?

FROST: Some people would say you've had more loved ones than most people.

(Laughter)

POWELL: Oh, happy day! Don't be jealous, don't be jealous.

FROST: I'm very happy, thank you. Do you think people would regard you as a greater leader if you'd apparently been an ascetic, or denied yourself all these creatures? "Creature comforts," perhaps I should say.

(Laughter)

POWELL: Why do you think the Roman Catholic Church is going through a catharsis now? Because the priests are looking for their creatures. There's a movement among the young priests that they want celibacy to be abolished. They want the creatures.

FROST: What we're talking about here is whether your rather lurid private life has affected the way your message is regarded, and whether people doubt how sincere you are?

POWELL: All right, let us answer that very factually. In the first place, I am the only chairman that the United States Congress has ever had, in writing from LBJ, from my beloved friend Jack Kennedy, from Speaker McCormack, I am the best chairman. I passed sixty laws without one defeat in six years.

Let's turn to preaching. When I preach, you better reserve your seat, and I will sell it to you, by the way.

FROST: I know. I didn't think it'd be free, coming from you.

POWELL: No, no.

(*Laughter*)

You're an Anglican, aren't you?

FROST: I'm an independent.

POWELL: But your family were Anglican.

FROST: No, my family were Methodists.

POWELL: Really?

FROST: My father was a Methodist minister.

POWELL: Congratulations. There's only one thing better than a Methodist. That's a Baptist.

FROST: Do you still call yourself a Baptist, or what?

POWELL: Second oldest church in New York City, I been there forty-one years.

Operating a church that costs one thousand dollars a day to operate. And my salary is five hundred and seventy-five dollars a month, with no fringe benefits.

FROST: No fringe benefits?

POWELL: Nope.

FROST: None at all?

POWELL: I will not allow them. They want to give me a car, they want to give me a house, they want to do this, they want to do that. Nope.

FROST: Just a little old island.

(*Laughter, applause*)

When you gave your first sermon—which, according to all the things written about you, was in 1932—

POWELL: No, sir.

FROST: No? Well that's what the books say.

POWELL: I'm not the book.

FROST: It said that you had the congregation weeping. What was the first text you ever preached from?

POWELL: My first sermon was on Good Friday in 1929. And my sermon was, "If You Walk a Mile," because that was the big billboard all across the nation. "If You Walk a Mile for a Camel." And I walked down this aisle for God. That was my first sermon.

FROST: And did you end with an appeal, like Billy Graham does, to people to come down the aisle?

POWELL: Who?

(*Laughter*)

FROST: William Graham.

POWELL: Oh, William—oh, yes, William.

FROST: Do you, like Billy Graham, appeal to people to come forward and commit themselves to God?

POWELL: Yesterday we baptized at the church all of the controlling group of the youth, female division, of the Black Panthers.

FROST: What do you think are the qualities that make you able to sway crowds? I asked Billy Graham that. What's your answer?

POWELL: I would say it's first sitting at the feet of a great man, my father, who was a great preacher. Secondly, paying my dues. I paid my dues, by the way. As my beloved friend Martin Luther King said from my pulpit, three months before he was assassinated, "Before some of us were born, some of us could walk, some of us could talk, Adam Powell was doing what we're doing now." The picketing, boycotting. Twelve years. Paid my dues.

So when I speak today, people say here's a man who's paid his dues.

FROST: But I read a quote that twelve days before Martin Luther King, your dear friend, was killed—

POWELL: Oh, we disagreed, oh yes.

FROST: —you shouted in a speech, "The day of Martin Luther King has come to an end!" Twelve days before he died.

POWELL: That's correct, that's correct.

FROST: Why did you say that?

POWELL: Because in my house in Bimini he confessed that he did not believe that total nonviolence was the answer any more.

FROST: I didn't know Martin Luther King as you obviously did, but I've read almost everything he said in his last year or so. You would agree, presumably, that he never espoused violence.

POWELL: When he finally gave up his position on total nonviolence, when he ascended in the pulpit of the Riverside Baptist Church, he said, "When I talk to my black people in the ghettos, and say that Molotov cocktails are not the answer, then they said to me, 'Martin Luther King, how can the United States of America become the greatest purveyor of violence in the world?'" And then Martin Luther King said, "After that I gave up my position on total nonviolence."

FROST: Yes, I would have said that while he feared that nonviolence might not succeed, he never took up any other sword.

What would be your definition of law and order?

POWELL: Law and order today is considered by many people a black boy running down the street mugging somebody, raping somebody, killing somebody. I want to know when this nation, that has no more customs guards today than when Calvin Coolidge was President, I want to know when this nation is going to get the big fat cats that run the narcotics and dope trade of the United States. When they going to nail one of them? That's law and order.

(Applause)

Law and order is: Who killed Medgar Evers, the president of the NAACP of Mississippi? Who killed—and it'll never come out in your lifetime—who killed my beloved friend, Jack Kennedy? The truth has not come out yet. That's law and order. That's law and order.

(Applause)

FROST: Do you know? Wait a minute.

POWELL: Who killed Martin Luther King? Where did Ray get the money from? Time magazine asked that two weeks in a row. Who killed Bobby Kennedy? That's law and order. We have had more assassinations in this nation in the past five years than the whole world has had in this century. That's law and order.

241

FROST: And on some of these things are you saying that you know the truth, or that the truth should be found?

POWELL: I know some of the truth. That's why they might get me next.

(*Laughter*)

They don't know that where the truth is—I have about ten people that know it and save it in safe deposit boxes.

FROST: What truth do you know?

POWELL: All right. You go to the library tomorrow morning and get the Warren Commission report. You'll get two volumes. You come to my office, and I'll tell my secretaries to let you see it. I got twenty-five volumes.

FROST: What, the full ones that were published, you mean.

POWELL: Jackie Kennedy's testimony. One half of her testimony was cut out of the Warren Commission report.

FROST: What are you saying was cut out?

POWELL: Go along, baby, go along, baby. Go along, sweetheart. Daddy loves you. The deputy sheriff of Dallas, sixteen points he made in his testimony. Cut out. The coroner that performed the autopsy on President Jack Kennedy's body at Bethesda United States Navy Medical Center went home that night and burned up his notes in his fireplace.

And if you got killed, or I got killed, or anybody here, those notes will be held in the files of the coroner's office for at least a month.

FROST: I know that there are a lot of terrible question marks surrounding the grassy knoll and all of that. But what are you saying? Do you have an alternative view of what occurred?

POWELL: I do not have the facts. But as a man of my age, sixty-one this year, forty-one years in the pulpit, a quarter of a century in Congress, I do now say publicly that there is a conspiracy in this nation. Who's financing it I do not know. But I think I'm on the right track.

FROST: What sort of conspiracy?

242

POWELL: Conspiracy to eradicate any man, black or white
—whether it's the white man who supported Gene McCarthy
in Chicago, or whether it's the blacks in North Carolina College, there's a conspiracy in this nation to eradicate or keep
down in some way—doesn't matter how—the voice of protest, which made America great.

We became great from protest. The *Mayflower* was a ship
of protest.

FROST: If there are facts that are not known, they obviously ought to be known.

POWELL: The archives have been sealed for half a century.

FROST: And if there is this conspiracy, then the people
ought to know about it.

POWELL: They can't.

FROST: But at the same time you must go a little further
with evidence. It is very attractive to take three or four things
that don't hang together properly and allege conspiracy. All
of us in a curious way want to believe that great men's deaths
have a meaning. It is horrible to think that great men's deaths
happen by chance, by a mad action or by a madman. A conspiracy is more attractive. It is also more attractive to us to
believe we know about a conspiracy that somebody else
doesn't.

So while I say that if there are facts that are not known, at
the same time it is terribly dangerous to spread thoughts of a
conspiracy. Unless you have facts to back it up.

(*Applause*)

POWELL: I have facts, I have facts.

Why would *Time* magazine ask in two consecutive issues,
"Where did Ray get the money from to kill Martin Luther
King?"

FROST: Good question. *Time* magazine obviously thought
there was an answer to that. But what evidence is there?

POWELL: They have it.

FROST: *Time* magazine has it?

POWELL: Yes. Why would you take a big capitalistic organ-

243

ization like Time-Life, Fortune, Sports Illustrated, and let them devote twelve pages this week to the pictures of the young men of America who were killed in one week? Why would they do that, a capitalistic organization? Pictures of young men that never had a chance to vote, never had a chance to look in the eyes of one of their babies.

FROST: That was a terribly effective issue, but come back to the question of James Earl Ray. What evidence do they have?

POWELL: What evidence? They have evidence that here is a man who had a white Mustang, here's a man who got through Canada—your part of the world, by the way—very easily. Here's an man who had the introduction to three people in Canada who looked like him. Here's a man who had the money to go from there to Portugal, and from there to your home town, London. Where did he get the money from? Ray didn't have the money.

FROST: I agree it's a mystery, but what evidence do you have that it was part of a payment from those organizing a conspiracy? I don't have the answer to that question. I think it's very fishy, too.

POWELL: Ah, thank you.

FROST: But I don't think I can go on to say I have evidence of a conspiracy, that's all. Unless you can give me more facts of where the money came from. Not "Where did he get it, where did it come from?"

POWELL: I know where it came from, and I will not tell you. But when we leave here, I'll tell you.

FROST: No, no, no. Don't let's have private chats. Let's talk to the people.

POWELL: No, no.

FROST: You said they've got a right to know. Tell them. (*Applause*)

POWELL: They have a right to know, like all of we Americans have a right to know many things that are kept from us. Here we are now. We passed a surtax on your income, ten percent more on your income tax.

FROST: You're getting away from the question.

(*Applause*)

POWELL: No, I'm not. I'm coming down the home stretch now, baby.

(*Laughter*)

We have billionaires in the United States. Clint Murchi son, Sr., just died. Hunt, Getty will get twenty-seven and a half percent of their billions of dollars off the top before they pay a tax. And that group is going to preserve their status quo, regardless of what it costs to do it. They do not want any-one, black or white, whether it's a Kennedy or a King, to come in and destroy their private financial power structure.

FROST: You're not suggesting, however, are you, that any of the men you've just mentioned is behind this conspiracy?

(*Laughter*)

Because (a) you'll need your lawyers, and (b) we'll need ours.

POWELL: I'll lend you four lawyers. I've been through a libel suit.

FROST: If you're saying it, then say it. But you're not say-ing that, are you?

POWELL: Shall I repeat it again?

FROST: No, answer my question. That's all. Are you saying that one of those men is responsible for this conspiracy?

POWELL: No. I'm just pointing out the picture in America.

FROST: Yes, but it's not facts, is it?

POWELL: It's a fact that twenty-seven and a half percent of your income you don't have to pay tax on, and you're a billionaire. That's a fact.

FROST: Oil depletion, and all that sort of thing.

POWELL: Yeah, and you don't want that changed.

FROST: Yes, but you're stopping being a hard-news man and becoming the gossip columnist again.

POWELL: Oh yeah, sure, Walter Winchell resigned. I took his place.

FROST: Can you name anybody who has anything to do with this conspiracy?

POWELL: No.

FROST: Because you don't know, or you can't say?

POWELL: I know, and I can say. But I have paid my dues, baby.

FROST: What is this "paid my dues"? If the people have a right to know, you have a duty to tell them. Share what you know.

POWELL: I haven't got any duty in life now except to live.

FROST: That's not the leader you started off talking about.

POWELL: No, that's my duty in life now, to survive and to live.

FROST: That's not Adam Clayton Powell, leader, that's Adam Clayton Powell, dilettante.

POWELL: I paid my dues. I've been out here forty-one years.

FROST: But how can you—?

POWELL: How old are you?

FROST: Thirty.

POWELL: All right, ten years before you were born I was out in the streets.

FROST: Paying your wretched dues, yes.

POWELL: Not wretched, but—

(*Applause, cheering*)

FROST: But if this is a terrible conspiracy—

POWELL: No wretched dues, don't call them wretched.

FROST: Well, they're getting more and more wretched every time we talk about them.

(*Applause*)

POWELL: No, no.

FROST: The thing is that if this is a great conspiracy, if it's rotting America, if it's an injustice, if it's what you're fighting, then you can't say, "I don't care, I've just got to live." If what you say is true, and you share what you know, you could change the course of current history. And you can't then just say, "I don't care."

POWELL: How?

FROST: If you named a group of people that are at the

246

center of the conspiracy you've alleged, and something was done about that conspiracy, and it prevented future assassinations, how dare you *not* say the name, if there is a name.

(*Applause*)

POWELL: Who is going to enforce anything that anyone says?

FROST: They will check the facts, and if they're true they will act.

POWELL: They got the facts, man. You know that.

FROST: All right. If they've got the facts and they're private, you make them public, and these people and the people at home will force them to act.

POWELL: It'd be on page twenty-six of the *New York Times*.

FROST: Rubbish. This is a democracy and it functions very well as a democracy.

POWELL: Oh, Lord have mercy.

FROST: In a situation like this the people's voice would be heard.

POWELL: The people's voice has been stilled in the land. The voice of the turtle cannot be heard.

FROST: Oh no. Please, if this is important and you know, speak. Either that, or it's unimportant, or you don't know. Which is it?

POWELL: I'll shut my mouth.

FROST: If you do know, and you're shutting your mouth, that's the most irresponsible thing you've ever done.

POWELL: I got a conscience to live with, that's true.

(*Groans from audience*)

FROST: But you just said now you didn't care about conscience. You said, "I just got to live."

POWELL: You can't live without a conscience.

FROST: I can only draw the conclusion that you do not have these facts, or you do not care.

POWELL: I would say at this stage of the game that I really don't care. I don't care.

FROST: That is a tragic admission.

247

POWELL: Yes, it is.

FROST: Those are very sad words to hear.

POWELL: I know it, sad for me.

FROST: I hope you'll rewrite them.

POWELL: Bless your heart. Keep the faith, baby.

Epilogue

◆

THAT'S IT. So many things that at this moment in time only an American could or would feel constrained to say in quite that way:

—"We became great from protest. The *Mayflower* was a ship of protest."
—"Nobody in this country really knows who his grandfather is."
—"Because the West is younger we haven't yet reached the stage where you ignore the man standing next to you at the bar."
—"If you asked me what's the one thing in the whole world I would like more than anything else, it's for even fifty seconds to be able to—pow—be in someone's head and just see the world through their eyes."
—"What's my daughter going to breathe in ten years?"
—"If we really worked at it with the technology that we have, in a few years we could destroy privacy as we know it."
—"I see no difference between a man who pushes cocaine at the beginning of *Easy Rider* and a man on Wall Street who's involved in a defense plant, who takes all of his money and puts it in a Swiss bank."
—"I love America and I don't think we've ever fulfilled our deepest dreams as a people."
—"We're beginning to understand each other in a day-

to-day way. And I just wish the adults would leave us alone for a while and let us try to work it out."

I am enjoying my voyage of discovery through America more than anything I can recall. If there were any readers who shared the view of some observers abroad that the Americans are an unself-critical people, they will have seen by now how wrong that is. The Americans analyze themselves ferociously, lacerate themselves mercilessly, refuse to believe they have found a final answer for anything.

Indeed, to friends and lovers of this country, the towering air of gloom sometimes seems unnecessarily thick. Of course there are towering problems. Ken Galbraith in one program reiterated his list of six: inequality, unequal economic performance, dependence on military spending, subordination to military power, industrial arrogance, and environmental damage—and that is quite enough for any country to hear from any critic.

However, America is also closer to the year 2000 than anywhere else on earth. And that means closer to the problems as well as to the excitement. As Arthur Schlesinger has said, "Every nation as it reaches a comparable state of technical development will have to undergo comparable crises. The present turmoil may be less the proof of decay than the price of progress."

It sems to me more than likely that the interaction of Americans' historic drive and aggressive self-help with the younger generation's search for a more compassionate society could produce fifteen years from now the most enlightened ruling generation the world has seen, rather than Armageddon.

In the meantime, everything about America will continue to be bigger than anywhere else—the problems and the inequalities, doubtless, but the achievements and the idealism, too.